Viktor Schauberger
A Life of Learning from Nature

Viktor Schauberger
A Life of Learning from Nature

Jane Cobbald

Floris Books

Viktor Schauberger (1885–1958)

First published in 2006 by Floris Books
© 2006 Jane Cobbald

British Library CIP Data available

ISBN-10 0-86315-569-3
ISBN-13 978-086315-569-7

Printed in Great Britain
By Biddles, King's Lynn

Contents

*This book is dedicated to Frau Ingeborg Schauberger,
a remarkable and determined lady who kept faith with
her father-in-law for over fifty years.*

Acknowledgments

Some good friends have helped me with this book. They include, in Australia, Jenny Mitchell; in Austria, Wolfgang and Susanne Prock, Johannes Stadler, Jörg and Ingrid Schauberger and Frau Ingeborg Schauberger; in Sweden, Curt Hallberg; and in the UK, Alick Bartholomew, Nick Raeside, Denise Tearle and Gill Whitehurst. My gratitude to you all, and particular thanks to my partner Nigel Thorley, who has been remarkably good-natured throughout this project.

As this book covers some contentious areas, there are bound to be differences of opinion about its content. For those, and any errors in the text, I take responsibility.

Jane Cobbald

A note to the reader:
Viktor Schauberger lived in the first half of the twentieth century, in a world with different values from today. One of the changes that has taken place since then is in the attitude to hunting. For his generation, it was part of the natural order of things that humans should hunt. He saw no contradiction between this and his huge respect for Nature. Nowadays, as the world is more complicated and many wildlife species are endangered, some of us are ambivalent about it. However, it is undeniable that many of his most extraordinary stories are from the times when he was out alone in the mountain forests, hunting.

A note on the illustrations:
This book contains a selection of drawings by Viktor Schauberger that have not been published before in book form. They are part of a series of sketches that he drew in the years 1946 and 1947. This was a difficult period for him, and his country. He was unable to continue with any of the projects

that he had previously been working on. He was isolated and housebound. Prevented from working on any outward, practical ventures, he turned inward. The drawings were made on lined paper and most of them had no accompanying text. For me, they allow a glimpse of the world as Viktor Schauberger saw it. They show his observation of the patterns in Nature, and his recognition of their significance. Some of them look like eddies in a stream; others like cogs in a machine. Still others could be interpreted either way. They are all part of a continuum, showing his fascination with the unending processes he saw at play around him. They demonstrate his motto: 'kapieren und kopieren,' comprehend and copy; in other words, first understand Nature and then copy it.

Abbreviations of Schauberger sources used in the text:
WW refers to *The Water Wizard*
NAT refers to *Nature as Teacher*
TFE refers to *The Fertile Earth*
EE refers to *The Energy Evolution*
Full details of these books can be found in the References and Further Reading section on p.163.

Foreword

by Alick Bartholomew

Viktor Schauberger made an extraordinary contribution to knowledge of the natural world. He is celebrated for his discoveries in the water sciences, in agricultural techniques, and in the energy domain — what enhances and what harms life. Schauberger provides us with a comprehensive and holistic approach to understanding Nature. Using Nature's cool methods, he invented energy generation devices to release people from enslavement to destructive sources of energy. He developed agricultural methods to enhance the quality of soil and crops.

Schauberger showed that when the natural ecosystems are in balance and biodiversity rules, there is great creativity and evolution of higher and more complex life forms, but there is also order and stability. When humans walked lightly on the Earth, we cooperated with Nature. While still part of her, we now behave as though we are superior, dominating other species and abusing the Earth's bounty. Viktor warned, eighty years ago, that if we continued to go against Nature, the Earth's eco-systems would become sick, the climate destructive and human society would break down, with extreme violence, greed and pandemic illnesses.

This is a very special book. From Jane's fascination with her subject comes a curiosity to discover how Schauberger's mind worked. For Viktor was an intuitive and a visionary — an engineer more than a natural scientist, whose preoccupation was to understand Nature's intriguing processes. Jane Cobbald has given us valuable insights into Viktor's worldview. She has skilfully worked his voice into the text, quoting anecdotes that give a flavour of his personality.

Most researchers learn from books what they to expect to see, and then observe what they unconsciously anticipated. Viktor

Schauberger did not have these expectations. He observed with fascination as does a child. Jane, with a woman's intuition, communicates this sense of wonder.

Her explanations of the importance of the right kind of motion, the most beneficial type of temperature change and the importance of egg shapes are very helpful. Her description of Viktor's insights into how plants grow, the subtle energies involved and the electromagnetic interactions in water and the soil help to demystify these processes.

After Viktor's death, his son Walter set up the Schauberger research institute, the Pythagoras Kepler School. Jane's conversation with his widow, Frau Ingeborg Schauberger, helps to bring alive the relationship between father and son.

Landscape healer and inventor of environment-friendly technology, Viktor Schauberger vividly described how our disdain for Nature's ways will bring only environmental catastrophe. His vision — of humanity working within Nature's laws — is the path we must rediscover, if we are to survive.

He had little ambition for himself, but with the understanding he acquired of how to live in harmony with our environment, he devoted his life to improving the lives of others. His insights are vital for us today when the prevailing scientific paradigm sees the Earth as inert matter and Nature is observed as a mechanical system, its resources exploited for humanity's benefit, contributing to the appalling desecration of the environment, and to climate change. Here, Jane Cobbald has produced a work that advances, at a very readable level, the understanding of the vastly important and relevant principles that Schauberger discovered.

Introduction

It was Viktor Schauberger's work with copper implements that first attracted me to his ideas. I grew up on a farm, and I remember registering an undercurrent of distress, a wondering whether humans' relationship to the earth and its creatures really has to be like this. I remember the sheep in the lambing sheds in spring. Sheep are still semi-wild, and although physically well cared for, the sheds did not seem to be the right place for them. The cultivated fields did not attract me either. The woods and wilder, less interfered-with parts of the farm were where I wanted to be.

I read about Viktor Schauberger as an adult, in the 1990s, and was inspired by the reports of his work with copper implements. It seemed such a simple yet elegant idea. Perhaps, after all, it was possible to find a different way of working with the earth.

I had to wait another ten years before I could pursue the idea any further. By then I had a garden, a typical English garden with flowers and vegetables. I was not a very successful gardener, although an enthusiastic one. Then I started using copper tools in my garden. As I worked with them, it gradually dawned on me that this felt very different. The tools slice into the soil with a clean cut. It feels as if one is working with the soil, not against it. In contrast, using my old iron tools made me feel that I had been imposing my will on the garden.

I will never forget harvesting my potatoes that first year. For several years I had tried to grow potatoes in small raised beds at the bottom of the garden, always with similar results. Each time I harvested slightly more potatoes than I had planted in the spring, and the ones I did harvest had all been burrowed through by slugs. This time it was a very different story. The plants had luxuriant growth, and by early August potatoes started peeping through the surface of the soil. I collected some of them to eat immediately, and earthed up the remainder with grass clippings. When I cleared the bed at the end of August, I had a bumper crop, with the yield approaching commercial levels. And of all of those potatoes, only six were eaten through by slugs. As I write this, I have just lifted this year's potato crop, and the yield is just as good as that first year. After the first season, I threw away all my old iron tools. I would not dream of using them in the garden now. I am still intermittently enthusiastic in my approach to gardening, but I have to say that it is more successful than it was. This is all highly subjective, and to make it even more so, I would say that the garden feels like a happier place now.

This book started as a piece of writing to myself. I was fascinated by Viktor Schauberger, and read all I could find about him. I started to look for the underlying principles, to try to fit together the different elements of his system in my head.

The following account is the result of that process. I look at Viktor Schauberger's descriptions of what he saw, his explanations of the processes he observed, and the inventions he developed as a result of his understandings. It is not a definitive explanation of Viktor Schauberger's ideas, but rather the results of my own meditations, based on Callum Coats' translations of the Schauberger archive and my own visits to the wild places, inspired by his writings.

My aim is to tease out the different strands of his system of thinking, and present them in his words. He coined new words and concepts to explain the natural processes that he observed. My sense is that Schauberger's explanations are not so much *difficult* as *different*. He came from first principles, the ways of Wise Nature, as he called it.

Many of his ideas take a different direction from mainstream science, and at times flatly contradict it. Where this happens, I follow Viktor Schauberger, although I refer to conventional science when it helps to explain his thinking.

Jane Cobbald, January 2006

I was drawn time and time again into the forest. I could sit for hours on end and watch the water flowing by without ever becoming tired or bored. ...

Gradually I began to play a game with water's secret powers; surrendering my free consciousness and allowing the water to take possession of it for a while. Little by little this game turned into a profoundly earnest venture, because I realized that one could detach one's own consciousness from the body and attach it to that of the water. When my own consciousness eventually returned, the water's most deeply concealed psyche often revealed the most extraordinary things to me. ...

By practising this blindfold vision, I eventually developed a bond with mysterious Nature, whose essential being I slowly learnt to perceive and understand.
Viktor Schauberger, Nature as Teacher, pp.29–30

1. The Making of a Water Wizard

Part of Viktor Schauberger's job as forest warden was to bring down timber from the mountain, which had already been sold. The usual way this was done was to have it hauled on sledges by teams of oxen. Schauberger hated to see the distress this caused to the beasts, under the burden of the difficult terrain, the load they had to drag, and the whip of their driver. He also knew that the driver had to load the sledge as heavily as possible, so that he could cover his expenses and make a living.

The track through the snow would be spoiled if the driver applied the brake-chains on the downhill sections, so he used to send the oxen careering downhill at a gallop, which should give them the momentum to breast the next rise. This put great stress on the animals, and on this particular occasion one of them collapsed. The driver got down and gave vent to his anger, whipping and shouting at the distressed animal to make it get up again. It struggled to get up, but was entangled in its harness. Schauberger shouted to the man to stop, but this only made him berate it more. He could see the animal's foaming mouth and the last of its crushed spirit glistening in its eyes.

The man then took out a halter with silver clappers, passed it over the backs of the standing oxen to the fallen one. When he fitted it over the ox's head, it took such fright that it made a last effort to stand up, and in the process knocked the man flying. This was the last straw for the driver. After he had recovered from his fall, he took a hammer, walked around to the sledge and knocked away the chains, so that the logs tumbled loudly away down the slope. He then led his team of oxen away.

After some thought, Viktor Schauberger now resorted to his preferred method of transportation, the one that he had been prevented from using until now. This was transportation by using the mountain streams. This method had been previously rejected for two reasons. First, it was said to damage the stream beds, and second, it was said that the heavier beech and pine logs would not float.

He knew that his father had transported many tons of beech logs by water over large distances. He remembered his father's explanation, that at night and especially in moonlight, water becomes fresh and lively, able to carry heavy logs with ease. He improvised a weir and sluice gate and had the scattered logs thrown into it. The following morning they floated downstream without difficulty, but as soon as the Sun's rays hit the water, they sank. By avoiding the daytime, Viktor Schauberger was able to bring almost all of the consignment down to the valley, with the exception of a few obstinate 'sinkers', which remained in a deep ravine.

Viktor Schauberger must have been a solitary child. He had several brothers and sisters, but it seems that he preferred to spend his time wandering in the woods near his home in upper Austria. His father, grandfather, and forebears as far back as could be traced, had worked in the forests. Young Viktor soaked up their traditions, and in his later life often made reference to the wisdom that had been passed on to him.

He was not an enthusiastic school pupil. His three older brothers went on to university, but when his father wanted him to follow their lead, Viktor refused. He had already noticed that too much book-learning prevented people from seeing the wonders that he was beginning to observe. He did not want to suffer the same fate, and was supported in this by his mother. It was agreed that he would train to become a state forest warden.

At the outbreak of the First World War he was twenty-four, and was called up. He fought in Russia, Italy, Serbia and France, and was eventually wounded. After the war he went to work for Prince Adolf von Schaumburg-Lippe, where he had responsibility for 21 000 hectares of almost untouched forest in upper Austria. In this large preserve, he was both forest warden and game warden.

In 1924 the Prince launched a competition to find the most efficient way to bring mature timber down from remote stands in the mountains. Viktor Schauberger had continued his observations of Nature, and presented his plans for a logging-flume, a water chute, based on his understandings. His starting point was to build a flume based on the way water wants to flow rather than on established ideas of flume design. As the design was so unorthodox, and as he was a simple forest warden with no formal training in these areas, it is perhaps not surprising that his proposal was rejected outright.

It was around this time that Viktor Schauberger came to the attention of the Princess, Prince Adolf's young wife, while she was hunting in his preserves on her birthday. With a dramatic sense of occasion he summoned a buck for her, a twelve-pointer, with the traditional Austrian huntsman's method of calling it by blowing on a conch-shell. After that memorable first visit, the Princess spent more time hunting in this large area, and Schauberger accompanied her in his role as game warden. On one such visit they discussed the competition, which had so far not yielded any useful results, and the conversation turned to Viktor Schauberger's own entry. The Princess asked for more details. Although the technical details were probably obscure to her, she could see that if it worked, it would be much cheaper than any of the other entries.

On her return, the Princess persuaded her husband to look at their game warden's unusual, but potentially profitable, design. An arrangement was arrived at. The design would be adopted on condition that Schauberger put up the funds. If it was successful, he would be reimbursed. For his part, he would have complete control of the design and construction of the flume.

To cut a long and eventful story short, Schauberger's logging flume was successful beyond even his own expectations. At that time, less than a decade after the end of the Empire, Austrian society was still strongly hierarchical. Taking this one opportunity offered by the Prince, Viktor Schauberger stepped outside his place in this rigid hierarchy. From then on, the pattern of his life departed from that of his ancestors.

This was when Schauberger first began to be known as the 'water wizard.' He left the employ of the Prince and went on to build similar installations all over central Europe. He was employed by the government in Vienna. An academic was assigned to work with him, to demystify his understandings for those with more conventional training. His work was published in academic journals. He patented several more inventions, for devices to improve water quality.

Even in earliest youth my fondest desire was to understand Nature and through such understanding to come closer to truth; a truth I was unable to discover either at school or in church.

Viktor Schauberger, NAT, p.29

As Viktor Schauberger's work became more widely known, it is perhaps not surprising that it also came to the attention of the Nazis. In 1934, Adolf Hitler invited him to Berlin. Hitler greeted him warmly, telling him that he had studied his work and was impressed by what he had read. Their allotted thirty-minute meeting lasted for an hour and a half. Showing the respect for truth and lack of consideration of vested interests that characterized him for all of his life, Viktor Schauberger proceeded to tell Hitler where his energy and river management policies had gone wrong. Hitler was concerned, and asked him to discuss this further with his scientific advisors. However, his subsequent meeting with the advisors was less productive.

This was the pattern of Viktor Schauberger's life in the nineteen-thirties. He was involved in a whirl of inventiveness. He submitted patents for energy generation devices. All the time he was supported by a few distinguished champions, and resisted by the weight of the Establishment. He was convinced that modern forms of energy generation were dangerous, destructive and poisonous, and that Nature operates by a different, constructive system of generation. It was his belief that through a deep understanding of the way Nature works, an alternative way would be revealed, that would be of benefit to the whole of life.

This was the situation at the outbreak of the Second World War. He was called up in 1941, although he was troubled by his wounds from the previous conflict and too old for active service. Viktor Schauberger left few records of what he did in that period, but it seems that he was obliged to continue his own researches in the service of Germany. In 1943 he was transferred to the SS. Under pain of death, he was obliged to work for Heinrich Himmler. He was given premises near Mauthausen concentration camp, and instructed to call on the inmates for his staff. He was able to extract some concessions: all those who worked with him were removed from the camp and allowed to wear civilian clothes. They set up their workshop at Schloss Schonbrunn, and after that was bombed by the Allies, set up a new one at the village of Leonstein in upper Austria.

At the end of the war, the Americans cleared his premises at Leonstein, while the Russians took everything out of his Vienna apartment, and then set fire to it. After the war he was imprisoned by the American forces for a few months. He was almost certainly questioned about his work, and advised not to proceed with it.

On his release, he turned his attention to a new area of enquiry, agriculture. He was still driven by the desire to find technologies that would improve the quality of life for human beings, and embody a more enlightened relationship with planet Earth. He conducted field trials with copper-plated agricultural implements, which led to remarkable results. However, once again he was prevented from making any commercial application of his ideas.

Having had another yet avenue closed off, he returned to his other researches, and finally received some endorsement from the academic Establishment. After the horrors of the last war, he was convinced that his inventions offered a way for the German-speaking people to redeem themselves in the eyes of the rest of the world. They could bring about a better world for all humanity.

It is likewise necessary to refine the current attitude of those, who as nature-alienated politicians, are to blame for (our) present lot, a situation for which the whole population is also doubtless culpable. Through the free and voluntary disclosure of Nature's greatest secret, this can in part be rectified.

Viktor Schauberger, May 1945, EE, p.91

The final episode of his life is a very sad one. In 1958 some Americans came to see him. They promised him all the facilities he needed, if he would come over to America to continue his researches. He had refused overseas invitations before, but for some reason he accepted this one. Viktor and his son Walter went over to the USA, although he spoke no English and Walter very little. Once there, the promised facilities never materialized. Viktor and Walter were on their own in a bungalow in Texas, with nothing to do. Viktor fell ill, and asked to return home. He was allowed to go, as long as he signed a document drafted in English by his hosts, relinquishing all rights to his present and future discoveries. He was an honourable man, so when he realized what he had agreed to, this meant that he could not continue his life's work. Within a week of his return he died, on September 25, 1958, in Linz, Austria.

2. The Winding Way to Wisdom

One day, when he was a young man, Viktor Schauberger saw something which stayed with him for the rest of his life. On the face of it, it was something that is not uncommon, that many of us have seen, but on this particular occasion the realization of its huge implications dawned on him, and gave him the inspiration for much of his future work.

He was in the high mountains, and was standing at the side of a stream. The stream was about a metre wide. It was crystal-clear, cold and fast-flowing. Various matters were troubling him, and had brought him to this spot. As a child, his mother had told him that the spirits of the departed return to such streams, and can provide guidance to the living in times of difficulty. She, also, would be there for him, she had said. Now, as a man, he felt in need of her help. He stared down into the water for some time, letting his gaze and awareness follow the stream, but no guidance came to him.

Disappointed, he gave up. He put his staff into the water to provide a lever to help him vault over to the other bank, and in so doing flushed a trout that had been motionless in the current. It darted away upstream in a flash. Several thoughts immediately occurred to him. When he disturbed it, it darted upstream, against the current, not downstream. What energy did it call on to do that? He realized he had seen such trout many times, almost motionless in these fast-flowing streams. How did they manage to stay still in the fast water, with only the odd flap of their gills and swish of the tail? And even more puzzling, Viktor Schauberger knew that not far downstream from where he was standing, there was a high waterfall. How had this trout got here in the first place?

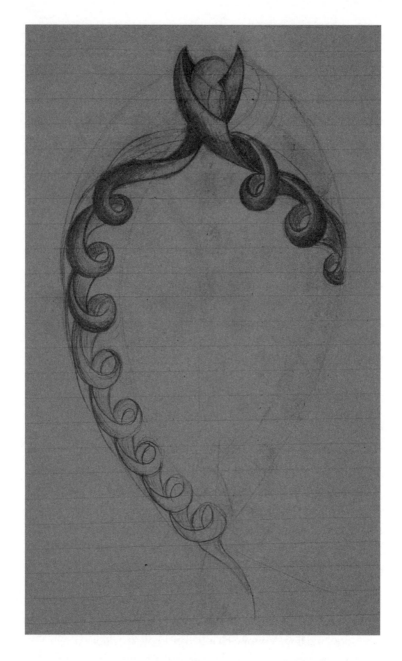

Untitled drawing by Viktor Schauberger

He realized that he was witnessing processes that conventional science does not consider. He began to have a glimmer of understanding about how they worked and how he could harness them for the benefit of humanity.

The spiral dance

One of Viktor Schauberger's favourite writings was the *Emerald Tablet* of Hermes Trismegistus, the early Greek alchemical text. It contains the famous maxim: *as above, so below.* Viktor Schauberger saw this principle at play in the movement of the Earth through the heavens, echoed in the flow of water in a stream.

Planet Earth spins on its axis. This gives us day and night. It also rotates around the Sun, at a tilted angle, so that at different times in the year, first one hemisphere and then the other receives the Sun's rays at a more direct angle. This gives us the seasons. And thirdly, the entire Solar System moves within the Galaxy, which gives us the astrological ages, known to the Ancients as Great Years. So our home planet spirals through the heavens, carrying us with her.

Liquids on the Earth's surface mirror this movement. On a much smaller scale, we can even see it as the water drains down a plughole. It naturally swirls around a central vortex. As we learnt at school, the draining water swirls anti-clockwise in the northern hemisphere and clockwise south of the equator. But next time you pull the bathplug, watch the central vortex itself. This also follows its own snakelike rhythm. So we see a double spiral, in a sense. The draining water swirls around the central vortex, and the whole also sways and moves.

The movement can be seen in the way a sycamore seed flutters through the air as it leaves the parent tree in autumn, spinning and spiralling to the ground some distance away. It is also reflected in dance, in the waltz. The partners circle around each other to the rhythm of the music, and also describe a larger circle as they move across the dance floor.

Now, picture yourself standing on a riverbank. Preferably a river that flows naturally, one that has not had its course altered by humans. Watch the flowing water. It does not flow at the same rate all over the river. It is fastest somewhere near the centre, and quite gentle, almost lapping, at the banks. Any bump or obstruction, such as a boulder, causes eddies to appear in the water downstream of it. These have their own spiralling motion, and a stick caught in one may temporarily reverse direction: upstream, against the current.

The current does not flow in a straight line — it snakes along, describing a wider arc. It spirals along downstream, like the water draining out of the bath or planet Earth spinning in the heavens. Eventually the entire watercourse migrates, and in wide river valleys we can see the meanders. On a smaller and much faster scale, we can watch rivulets on the beach as they scurry on their way to the sea, and their meanders move across the sand.

Viktor Schauberger said that a body of water in its watercourse attempts to mirror the three types of motion of the planets. First, the water rotates about its own axis: CYCLOID motion, like the planet's spinning on its axis to give us day and night. Then, the water SPIRALS along as it flows in its bed, as planet Earth spirals around the Sun in the course of the year. And finally, the entire watercourse twists and turns in a SPACE-CURVE, mirroring the entire solar system as it follows its path through the galaxy. This is why water when left to its own devices never flows in a straight line.

His great insight was to take this thought one step further — that water is at its most healthy and potent when it is able to flow as it wants to. He applied his insight to practical applications. The logging-flumes that he built were designed to encourage the water to flow in this way, and so were able to transport logs that were heavier than water. The layout of the logging-flumes was designed to stimulate this *cycloid-spiral space-curve* motion.

One day, young Viktor Schauberger was sitting on the bank of one of the Od lakes in Upper Austria. It was a still, hot summer afternoon, and he was debating whether to have a swim.

As he was sitting there, he noticed some movement in the lake water. It started to swirl, with no apparent cause. Trees, which had been carried down to the lake in the spring thaw and become lodged in the sand of the edges of the lake, began to be dislodged by the swirling water. They were carried towards what now looked like a whirlpool in the centre of the lake. There, they stood on end and were dragged down, with such force that their bark was stripped off. The trees did not reappear.

All was calm again, but only for a short while. The lake began to emit rumbling noises, which grew louder, building up into a bellow. Then, with a thunderous roar, a waterspout rose from the centre of the lake. It twisted and funnelled above the lake surface, as tall as a house.

Then it collapsed. Waves struck the shore, forcing him to retreat from where he had been sitting. When they settled, the water level of the lake was noticeably higher.

This phenomenon was known to the locals. They said that after a long period of hot weather, the lakes start to rumble, then they produced these water spouts.

Gravity and levity

The Sun is by far the largest and heaviest object in the solar system. Why don't all the planets fall towards it? Because they are moving around it. Something in their movement prevents them from falling towards the Sun. Closer to home, both trees and people grow upwards, against the pull of gravity. Something enables them to resist gravity. Viktor Schauberger refers to this opposing force as LEVITY. As we know from the experiences of astronauts, the pull of gravity weakens the higher one rises above the atmosphere. This would suggest that it also is not constant.

Picture a spinning-top. As it spins, it stands on its point, in apparent defiance of gravity. Once the spinning stops, it falls down. As the top spins, it does not stay in a single place like a ballerina. It moves along the surface, describing a larger spiral. In other words, it moves in an approximation to a cycloid-spiral space-curve.

Now, imagine a drop of water resting on the surface of the spinning-top. When the top begins to spin, the droplet will fly off. What if the water is inside the spinning-top, like water inside the earth? It will be caused to rise.

I think it would have been very much better, had Newton contemplated how the apple got up there in the first place.

Viktor Schauberger, NAT, p. 90

This levitational force concentrates towards the core, to the vortex at the centre of the spiral. It has powerful expression in a tornado. With a tornado, the mass of falling air and water causes the formation of a central vortex. It acts like a giant vacuum cleaner, carrying large objects over a considerable distance — yards, and at times, even miles. Because water, when it is moving as Nature intended, moves in a cycloid-spiral space curve, it contains levity in its movement. This process might explain how a trout can leap up a waterfall, as the fish moves into the uplifting centre of the spiral of descending water.

If it is prevented from moving in this way, the levity is lost and the water is flat. This is true of groundwater rising inside the Earth, sap rising in a tree, and a river flowing towards the sea. Such water nourishes and sustains the life in it. In a fast-flowing stream, have a look at some water plants. In the fast current they wave gently, upright, more as if they were caught in a breeze than by the torrent rushing over them. The only time that such plants are uprooted is when the stream goes out of control and loses its rhythm — in a flood, for example.

It was Spring, during the spawning season, on a bright moonlit night. Viktor Schauberger was sitting beside a pool at the base of a waterfall. The water fell like liquid metal into the pool, then rippled and settled. The angle of the moonlight on the water allowed him to see the circling fish in the clear water of the pool.

Suddenly, all the fish scattered. A large trout then appeared in the pool from downstream. It started to swim in a loop. As it swam, its movements became more pronounced, like a figure-of-eight. It seemed to Viktor Schauberger that this trout was almost dancing a reel. Its dance took it under the swirling water at the base of the waterfall.

It disappeared. All Schauberger could see was some wild spinning water, above the spot where he had last seen the trout. The next moment it was there again, but standing on its tail and floating upwards with no apparent effort. It reached the top of the waterfall, and he caught sight of its tail fins as it did a quick back-flip. He heard the loud smack as it landed on the water beyond the waterfall.

More about motion

Viktor Schauberger describes the above process as PLANETARY MOTION or ORIGINAL MOTION. It is a cool, concentrating, centripetal movement, drawing inwards to the centre of the spiral. The mechanical inventions of the Industrial Revolution were based on the reverse of this process. Our machines spiral outwards, causing noise, heat and pressure. Such machines are known to be inefficient. Inside an engine the components, often including fossil fuels, meet in the medium of fire. They are destroyed to produce energy or movement, and release poisonous waste products.

Schauberger refers to this kind of movement as TECHNO-ACADEMIC or TECHNICAL motion: *techno* from the Greek word *tekhno-*, meaning skill or craft, implying a work of artifice; *academic* because it is taught in all academic institutions.

This kind of motion is based on pressure, spiralling outwards. As well as producing force, technical motion leads to heat, expansion and the destruction of the components. Schauberger says Nature only uses this motion to cause decomposition. This principle has been applied in everyday life. Jars of preserves usually have a 'safety button' in the centre of the lid, with a message not to use the contents if the button can be depressed. If the contents have started to decompose, they expand, and so the safety button pops out.

Today's technology strives to move forwards with forces that operate backwards.

Viktor Schauberger, EE, p.174

As with all energy, there is a radiation associated with each form of motion. Standing next to an engine, one can almost feel it. Viktor Schauberger says that if it is sent through a vacuum tube, a dark red light can be seen. This emanation leads to a deterioration in the quality of our water, our food and even our thought processes. He views water as the living blood of a living Earth, and says that water which is forced to move technically, through a turbine for example, can become diseased, even carcinogenic. Viktor Schauberger tells us that the ancient Greeks were aware of this technology, but unlike us, they refused to use it. They thought it was too dangerous, preferring to rely on people- and animal-power for their physical work.

It was either an abysmal stupidity or the greatest crime
of all time to exploit decomposive atomic energies for the
build-up of a world-wide economy.

Viktor Schauberger, EE, p.27

Original motion can also be felt. Who has not felt refreshed
and calmed, after spending some time on a riverbank, watching
the water wind its way towards the sea? This motion promotes
a blue-green energy which diffuses outwards, enhancing to all
life and increasing the soil fertility in the surrounding land.

Whereas techno-academic motion causes pressure as the
components meet and explode, original motion has the opposite effect, as they meet and condense. Their interaction leads
to a reduction in pressure, which Viktor Schauberger describes
as a BIOLOGICAL VACUUM. He applied this principle in several
of his inventions.

'How else should it be done then?' is always the imme-
diate question. The answer is simple: Exactly in the
opposite way that it is done today!

Viktor Schauberger, NAT, p.11

Watching a stream tumbling down the mountainside, is the
water pushed or pulled? Are the pebbles and stones pushed or
pulled along the streambed? Viktor Schauberger would say that
they are pulled, just as water is drawn down the plughole. He
refers to this as TRACTIVE FORCE. In the same way, he would say
that planet Earth falls through the heavens.

It would seem obvious that a watercourse's ability to carry
heavy loads depends on its gradient. The steeper the gradient, the greater the carrying capacity. Viktor Schauberger
questioned this conventional wisdom. As his logging flumes
showed, the tractive force associated with original motion has

an equal or greater carrying capacity to a steep gradient, and does not cause turbulence or destroy the watercourse in the process.

Birds and fish, whose bodies are designed to process the same levitational energies, are drawn through their medium as they move. Here again, we see the converse of the technology that runs all of our machines. Technical motion repels and pushes. Original motion invites, attracts, draws along.

A bird does not fly — it is flown. A fish does not swim — it is swum.

Viktor Schauberger, NAT, p.175

In the same way, Viktor Schauberger asserts that in the human body, it is not the heart that pumps the blood, but the blood that pumps the heart. In support of this, he says that when the blood is overheated, as for example when a person has a fever, the heart is affected and its rhythm of beating changes.

There was a fish-eagle that used to visit one of the mountain lakes. Every evening at about the same time it appeared above the lake, circled over it uttering its eerie cry, plummeted down to the water, then flew away clutching a salmon in its claws. There was a mystery for the young Viktor Schauberger. Salmon are not surface swimmers. How did the fish eagle catch them without getting its feet wet?

At one side of the lake there was a rocky promontory with a tall spruce tree growing on it. One evening, he climbed the tree. He stayed still, hidden in the foliage, watching through his telescope. He could see the salmon swimming in their hole below him, not far away. He kept an eye out for the eagle.

Punctual as usual, it arrived over the lake. It gave a shrill cry, announcing its presence to all in the valley. It then began to fly upwards, spiralling above the lake in ever-decreasing circles. Suddenly, it dropped like a stone to the lake, then braked just above the surface with a flap of its wings. It already had a large salmon wriggling in its claws. It flew away with its catch, over the forest.

Viktor had been so mesmerized by the eagle that he had forgotten to watch what the salmon were doing. He resolved to watch everything next time.

When he was able, he went back to the tree on the promontory overlooking the lake. There were the salmon, swimming in their hole. Again, in the early evening, the fish eagle announced its arrival with a shrill screech. It then began its spiralling flight above the lake. This time, Viktor watched the salmon closely, and was so hypnotized by their movement that he nearly fell off his perch and out of the tree. The salmon swam in the same spiral, mimicking the movement of the fish eagle above them. As they rose in the water, in imitation of the eagle's upward flight, they swam closer and closer together, towards the surface. The fish in the middle of the spiral were so close to each other that their fins eventually broke through the surface of the water. Down it came. Its shadow appeared over this miniature maelstrom, and a second later it flew away with a salmon in its clutches.

Viktor went back to watch this drama many evenings. The fish eagle always arrived on time, and uttered its echoing screech. Every time, he felt himself swaying in his tree, as all of the players were moved in the same spiral. And nearly every time the fish eagle flew away with a salmon in its claws.

3. Feeling the Earth's Pulse

There was a spring on a high mountain plateau, covered by a ramshackle little building. As this domed stone hut looked as if it might fall down at any time, Viktor Schauberger, the keen young forest warden, decided to have it demolished. His older hunting companions, however, did not think this was a good idea. 'If you take the hut down,' they said, 'the spring will dry up.'

Although he could not see any logic in this, Schauberger decided to proceed more carefully. He asked his men to number each stone as they dismantled the hut, so that it could be rebuilt if necessary. This was done.

As the older men had foretold, the spring indeed dried up. This plateau had few sources of water, and the spring was valuable. On his instructions, the cupola was rebuilt, and after a few days, water began to flow again.

From this experience, he realized that there was a sensitive relationship between sunlight, heat and groundwater, which he did not yet fully understand.

The anomalous liquid

Water temperature is a critical part of Viktor Schauberger's system. It is well known that water is an unusual substance, in that it is denser in its liquid than its solid state. This is why ice floats on the surface of a body of water. In fact, water is at its densest at four degrees Celsius, just above freezing. Schauberger refers to this temperature as the anomaly point or point of indifference. He also says that water at this point is temperature-less.

The Earth is permeated with water, which feels the pulses of changing temperatures from the rhythms of the days and the seasons. These rhythms of warming and cooling diffuse down into the Earth. And in response, the groundwater itself constantly changes temperature. Just as meteorologists compile charts for air temperatures, drawing a line between all points with the same temperature, a similar chart could be drawn for the groundwater, showing strata at the same temperature. It is warmed from below, and alternately cooled and warmed from above. Somewhere beneath our feet, there is a stratum which is at the anomaly point. Schauberger describes this as the BOUNDARY LAYER.

Now we come to a stunning insight. Any piece of water that is moving away from the anomaly point, either warming towards five degrees or cooling towards three degrees, will expand. When something expands, it moves outwards in all directions. All directions, including towards the water at the anomaly point. This means that the boundary layer is continually squeezed by the expanding water around it, like toothpaste in a tube. As long as the cap is off, a slight pressure at the base of the tube sends the toothpaste out of the nozzle, the point of least resistance around the mass of toothpaste.

Conversely, any water that is cooling or warming towards the anomaly point, contracts as it becomes denser. This draws in more water behind it. So the stratum of water at the anomaly point of four degrees Celsius is the most dense, and is buoyed up by all of the water around it.

Everything flows, floats and moves. There is no state of equilibrium — there is no state of rest.

Viktor Schauberger, WW, p. 167

There is a pulsating rhythm in the groundwater below us, expanding and condensing as it responds to changing temperatures through the days and seasons. With the levitating effect of the Earth's movement, it gradually rises upwards. If the vegetative cover is removed, then the soil is exposed to the heat of direct sunlight, and the resulting pulse of warmth sends the water table back down again. As long as the surface is protected by vegetation and kept at a constant temperature, the temperature-less water will eventually break through.

Viktor Schauberger on many occasions measured the temperature of springwater as it emerges from the ground, and found that the water in mountain springs is indeed at or near a temperature of four degrees Celsius. At the high springs, it emerges at this temperature all year round. These springs also flowed most strongly in daytime, in summer, when the Earth has warmed and squeezed the temperature-less layer.

In any body of water, the boundary layer is buoyed up by the pressure from the surrounding water: cooling or warming but, nevertheless, expanding. This is another part of the explanation of how Schauberger's logging-flumes were able to carry logs that were heavier than the water which was transporting them. In his logging-flumes, he let out used water at certain points, and fed in fresh, cool water so that this process could continue all along the flume.

A body of water also responds to the rhythm of day and night, warming during the day and cooling at night. Schauberger says that the foresters traditionally transported the heaviest logs downstream at night, when the water has its greatest carrying capacity.

Viktor Schauberger had many disagreements with the Establishment, as he promoted his unorthodox ideas. However, he also had support from some unexpected quarters. One such supporter was the Agriculture Minister, Andreas Thaler, himself the son of a farmer. Thaler told him the following story.

'In the vicinity of my farmhouse in the Tyrol runs a spring, which I always observed with some anxiety during hot weather because this little spring was the be-all and end-all for myself and my farm. In this way, year after year, I was able to establish that this little spring discharged higher and higher up as everything around it began to dry up and turn brown. The hotter it was, the colder the water became, and eventually during an extremely dry summer it emerged about twenty paces higher up. The water was better and there was more of it.' (NAT, p.67)

Later, Schauberger encountered another wandering spring, similar to the one on Minister Thaler's farm, in the mountains of Montenegro. His guide told him that in summer it emerged high up the mountainside, and in winter, its flow diminished, it started in the valley below. Viktor Schauberger took out his thermometer and measured the temperature of the emerging springwater. It was exactly 4 degrees C. Fifteen metres downstream, the water was already warmer, at 8 degrees C.

Water at the anomaly point has the greatest carrying capacity, because in itself it is dense, and is supported by the surrounding water. It can carry the most solids in suspension, and gases in solution. This water is ripe. It is ready to give up its goodness to the surroundings. Springwater is rich with the carbon compounds it has gathered in its upward journey. These carbon compounds come from the remains of the ancestors of the vegetation now flourishing on the surface. As the water warms on contact with the sunlight, it will give them up. Hence, in a bottle of high-quality, just-bottled springwater, we see little bubbles forming on the sides. These are of carbon dioxide, as the carbon in the springwater mixes with atmospheric oxygen. Not quite the same as carbonated mineral water. If the water is taken to a cool, dark location, such as a cellar, then it will reabsorb the bubbles, but the water will taste flat and insipid. It has lost that initial sparkling, wholesome quality which it acquired in its upward journey through the Earth.

Viktor Schauberger believed that temperature explains why sometimes a carcass in the water floats to the surface, bloated, and other times they sink, never to reappear. In the first instance, the body has been heated, expanded and started to putrefy. In the second, it sinks to the boundary layer, where it is gradually reintegrated into the Earth's energy store. In the first instance, the carcass has been moved technically: winding outwards, expanding, and has heated up; in the second, it has cooled and moved planetarily: inwinding, condensing and cooling. When we wash in warm water, we are relying on this property of heated water to break things down. Washing in cold water may be stimulating, but it doesn't remove the dirt so effectively. Each process has its place.

Whether growth or decline takes place is exclusively a question of temperature ... It endows water with its utterly essential energy form. In one case this signifies growth or life, and in the other, decline or death.

Viktor Schauberger, TFE, p. 68

Temperature gradients

Viktor Schauberger introduced a new concept to explain the properties of water as it changes temperature: the concept of TEMPERATURE GRADIENTS. Water moving away from the anomaly point, either by warming or cooling, is on a negative temperature gradient. As it moves away, it gives up some of the goodness it has gathered. Water which approaches the anomaly point, growing more dense and gathering into itself from the surroundings, is on a positive or falling temperature gradient. It is as if water on a negative temperature gradient is breathing out, and on a positive temperature gradient it is breathing in.

                                                    15.10.1941

Lieber Walter !

Im Anhang zu gestrigen Brief,kannst Du Dr. Carl sagen,dass ich den ver-
sautesten Flusslauf in Ordnung bringe,auch Flüsse,die zu kleines oder
zu grosses geologisches Gefälle haben.-

J e d e r Fluss muss individuell behandelt werden,wenn zwar im grossen
und ganzen für alle das natürliche Schema f gilt,so muss doch j e d e r
Fluss untersucht werden,an w e l c h e r Krankheit er leidet.-

Du kannst mit ihm meinetwegen jeden Vorschlag annehmen,allerdings behalte
ich mir jede Betrugsabsicht vor.-Denn auf diesem Gebiete habe ich aller-
hand erlebt.-

Die natur-nahe Flussregulierung ist so einfach,dass ein einziges Beispiel
genügt,um selbst einen heutigen Wasserfachmann die Schuppen von den natur-
unverbundenen Augen zu nehmen.-

Ich müsste es ablehnen,nur für den Anleiter behandelt zu werden und dann,
wenn die Leute einmal sehen,um w a s es hier geht,einen Fusstritt zu
bekommen.-

Ich brauche für meine Regulierungsart keine Ingenieure,kein Projekt,sondern
nur einige gute Stein-und Holzarbeiter,die überall zu finden sind.-

In meinen Flüssen gibt es keine Hochwasserschäden,keine Anrisse,keine
Unterkolkungen und fast keine Nachreparatur mehr.-Die mildesten Flüsse
werden frisch und lebendig kühl und rein und die wildesten Flüsse zahm.-
Auch die heutige Wildbachverbauung ist absolut naturunrichtig und daher
falsch.- Also verhandle auf welcher Basis immer mit Dr.Carl.-Wenn ich
nicht abermals betrogen werde,ist mir jeder Passus recht,der sich inner-
halb den Rahmen bewegt,den ich Dir Gestern schrieb.- Denn umsonst ist
nicht einmal der Todt zu haben,und wird daher nichts ungebührliches ver-
langen,was auch bei mir nicht der Fall ist.-

                                    Besten Gruss Dein

Letter from Viktor Schauberger to his son, 1941

Temperature is thus the difference between differences, out of which the ceaseless motion of evolution arises, which is itself the product of tensions resulting from the contrasting directions of movement.

Viktor Schauberger, EE, p.3

Temperature gradients help us to understand why the soil sometimes absorbs rainwater, and sometimes it runs off on the surface. Bare soil absorbs warmth from the sunlight. When it is warmer than the falling rainwater, the water in the ground is expanding at a faster rate than the falling rain. So there is a negative temperature gradient from the Earth to the air. This is enough to prevent the rainwater from penetrating into the soil, and so it runs away along the surface. In hot, arid lands, this leads to flash floods after rainfall. The rain cannot penetrate the hot ground, and so runs away on the surface.

When the soil is covered with vegetation, this protects it from the direct heat of the Sun, and so it stays cool. In this case, there is a positive temperature gradient. The warm rainwater expands into the ground, where it is cooled, thus allowing more rainwater to be absorbed.

The movement of water down the rivers to the sea, into the air by evaporation and back to the earth as rain is known as the HYDROLOGICAL CYCLE. Schauberger adds a new dimension to the standard understanding of this cycle, by describing the full and half hydrological cycles. When the ground is cool enough to absorb it, the rainwater completes its full cycle of going through the Earth, maturing and appearing at springs. It then flows into rivers and streams, evaporates, forms into clouds and falls again as rain. He calls this the full hydrological cycle. When the cover of vegetation has been removed, water is prevented from entering the ground and so runs off on the surface. It then evaporates again, to eventually fall as rain. In other words, the water takes a short cut, missing the section of its journey through the earth.

He described this second process as the half hydrological cycle. This water can be drinkable, but is not so mature or beneficial as water that has completed the full cycle.

Temperature and the rivers

The concept of temperature gradients also helps us to understand what is at play when a river flows quietly in its course, and what causes it to eat into its banks, silt up or flood. The part of the water which is the nearest to the anomaly point is where the current is strongest. This water flows fastest. Schauberger called it the core water-body. When the river is flowing smoothly and quietly, the core water-body winds into itself from the surrounding, warmer water, thereby cooling it and relieving any pressure on the riverbanks.

If the cover of vegetation is removed from the banks, more sunlight hits the water surface, and so there is more work for the river to do, to manage this extra heat. Artificial concrete banks can be rough, causing frictional heat as the water flows past. When a river is straightened, this means a steeper gradient, which it also has to deal with.

Temperature gradient also governs the quality of silt on the riverbanks. The core water-body, being closest to the anomaly point, has the greatest carrying capacity. So the largest stones are carried in this part of the river. As the water warms towards the banks, progressively finer particles are deposited. The banks themselves are sealed with the finest sediment, which acts as a skin for the river.

This understanding led Schauberger to see the folly of attempting to control a river by straightening it or shoring up its banks. It was back-to-front thinking, in his view. The river controls the bank, not the other way around. He was clamorous in his criticism of the water authorities. He published letters and articles accusing them of destroying the Rhine and Danube, turning what had been the glory of central Europe into poisonous channels of sludge, losing many acres of valuable farmland in the process. This barrage of abuse from an ex-forester with no academic training did not endear him to the decision-makers.

A river, when it is left to its own devices, will regulate itself. It will even modify its own gradient, to enable it to flow at the optimum speed. Where it falls steeply, there is increased friction both between the layers of water in the river and with the bed and banks. This means more heat, so the water warms up. This causes the water to deposit some of the sediment it is carrying. This in turn reduces the gradient, and so the river can flow more coolly and peacefully. Further downstream, the cooled core water-body can now take up more sediment. And so it continues, breathing in and out, all the way to the sea.

Some practical applications

Man-made constructions had a place, he believed, as long as they took account of the way water wants to flow and respond to its environment. In 1927 he submitted, and was eventually granted, a patent for river-regulation devices to regulate a river's flow from within. These took the form of concrete blocks, which are anchored to the riverbed at intervals along its course. The inner surfaces of the blocks are curved, forming the profile of the inside of an egg. They are scored with runnels leading inwards and upwards in an increasing curve, towards the centre of the flow of the watercourse. These brake-groins, as he called them, are installed upstream of where the river is eating into its bed. The purpose of these blocks is to direct the water flow towards the core water-body, away from the riverbank. When such blocks are installed, the river is able to carry heavier rocks and sediment past the brake-groin, and deposit them a little further downstream.

Another area he turned his attention to was dam construction. Temperature gradients are critical for the safety of dams.

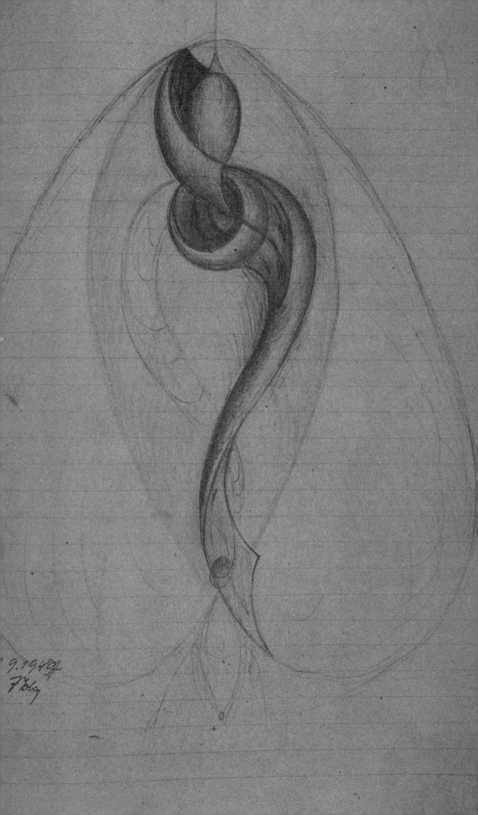

If the concrete dam wall is warmer or cooler than the water it retains, the difference in temperature means that the two bodies will interact. The temperature gradient determines whether the water held back by the dam will eat away at it, causing cavities in the wall, or deposit sediment on it, thereby strengthening it. In 1930, Viktor Schauberger designed a dam wall that took these properties of water temperature into consideration and turned them to advantage. When the surface of a lake freezes in winter, the warmer water, at four degrees Celsius, is trapped at the bottom. He proposed that there should be a second skin on the inner side of the dam wall, facing the lake, with an opening between these two skins at the top and bottom. At the base of the dam, the warmer water from nearer the lakebed is drawn into the gap between the two skins. It rises and eventually trickles over a lip at the top of the dam. The water that is in contact with the concrete dam wall is warmer than the surface water and the surrounding air. With less marked extremes of temperature, the dam wall structure does not deteriorate so rapidly. In summer, the temperature difference is reversed. The bottom-water is now cooler than the surface water, and as it is drawn upwards it cools the dam wall. The same design now has the opposite effect, protecting the dam wall from overheating. In both cases there is a positive temperature gradient towards the dam wall, as the temperature of the dam wall is nearer to the anomaly point than the surface water in the lake. Consequently, the lake water does not eat into the dam wall. This mechanism also protects the dam from the fluctuation in temperature between day and night. This simple design protects the entire dam wall from the extremes of temperature that would otherwise inevitably damage its structure.

The design also allows the engineers to regulate the temperature of water flowing out of the dam. Water can be drawn off at different levels in the lake, depending on the time of year and the temperature of the natural watercourse. This allows the

◄ *Untitled drawing by Viktor Schauberger*

river downstream to flow at its optimum temperature, reducing turbulence and preventing it from eating into its banks or silting up as it tries to accommodate the introduced water of a different temperature.

All that is necessary to re-establish the natural world order, is to regulate the anomaly state of health by means of the temperature gradient.

Viktor Schauberger, TFE, p.34

A new friend

This period of the early 1930s was one of the rare occasions when Viktor Schauberger had the support of a respected academic. Professor Philipp Forchheimer, a retired hydrologist, was assigned to accompany him, initially to understand and explain the mysterious logging flumes. Prof Forchheimer must have been a patient and open-minded man. He was able to follow Viktor Schauberger's line of reasoning and see the sense in it. He became so convinced of the validity of Viktor Schauberger's insights, that he arranged for him to write a series of articles, which he himself edited, for the Austrian *Journal of Hydrology*. Forchheimer himself wrote: 'The superiority of the Schauberger design over contemporary designs is apparent.' (WW, p.133)

This was quite a step for a man of Forchheimer's stature and reputation. He put himself in the role of a student, and was able to see past Viktor Schauberger's disdain and intolerance of academics to the truth of what he was saying. He recognized the importance of his understandings and championed them to his colleagues.

For his part, the conversations with Forchheimer's colleagues confirmed for Schauberger what he had already suspected. He and the scientists had a fundamentally different perception of the nature of water and what that means. For him, the starting point, inspired by his intuitive insights and confirmed by many experiences, is that water is a living entity. This means that it has a structure and a character. It breathes, and goes through processes of dying and renewal. It can be healthy or unhealthy. His focus was to understand how the processes of life manifest through water, and how we can work with these processes for the benefit of all. For the scientists he met, water was an inert substance with some interesting physical properties. Schauberger's viewpoint meant that he was unable to meet the scientists on their terms, or even halfway. He saw a living world; they studied a mechanical one.

Were water actually what hydrologists deem it to be — a chemically inert substance — then a long time ago there would have been no water and no life on this Earth.

Viktor Schauberger, WW, p.85

Meeting a man of Philipp Forchheimer's stature, learning and open-mindedness was fortunate indeed. However, Forchheimer was an old man, and he died in 1931. The series of articles, which was part way through, was terminated, and the drawbridge from the mainstream scientific community was raised once more.

I regard water as the blood of the Earth. Its internal process, while not identical to that of our blood, is nonetheless very similar. It is this process that gives water its movement. I would compare this inner motion, the origin of all possible physical movement, to that of a blossoming flower bud. As it unfolds, it creates a vortex-like

crown of petals, in the centre and at the end of which
stands the true secret of motion — life in statu nascendi,
in the form of a concentration of movement.

Viktor Schauberger, WW, p. 85

Viktor Schauberger marvelled at the way a dewdrop
forms. Before the Sun rises, there is a short interval in
which the air seems to grow cooler. In this moment, if
the conditions are right, an embryonic sac, like an empty
soap-bubble, appears at the tip of a blade of grass. In the
cool, blue, high-intensity early morning light, the bubble
fills with water. Were a person to walk barefoot on the
dew-soaked grass at this point, they would feel energized
and invigorated. As the Sun rises higher in the sky, the
quality of light changes, warms, and its rays directly
touch the dewdrop. At this moment, the soon-to-be-
born dewdrop is united with its soul. The dewdrop now
feels the force of gravity and so grows heavier, bending
the blade of grass. The sac bursts and the water trickles
down the leaf, transferring its goodness to the Earth.

4. Eggs and Egg-shapes

The first logging flume that Viktor Schauberger con-
structed, for Prince Adolf of Schaumburg-Lippe, was
unlike any other logging flume seen before. It was made
of wood, it snaked around the mountainsides rather than
following the shortest route, and it had the profile of the
blunt end of an egg. He had stumped up the money for
the construction himself, so his bank balance as well as
his self-respect were riding on the success of this venture.

The day came when he felt ready to give the flume a
preliminary test. The first log was taken from the stack
and introduced into the mouth of the flume. It floated for
about a hundred yards, then sank to the bottom. The water
backed up behind it and overflowed at the sides of the
flume, but the log did not budge. Schauberger was aghast.
He had the log removed and sent his workers away, so that
he could ponder the problem in peace and quiet. He looked
a little more closely and came to the diagnosis that the gradient was too steep for the low volume of water.

He walked slowly alongside the flume. He was sure
that the curves were correct. He reached the holding pool
further down, sat on a projecting rock in the warm sun-
shine, and looked down into the water. As he sat there,
he felt something scrabbling through his leather trousers.
He leapt up, turned around, and saw that he had been
sitting on a snake that had coiled up on the warm rock.
He picked it up and threw it into the water. It swam to
the bank, but couldn't get out because the rock face was
too steep. It swam back and forth, and eventually made
its way right across the front of the dam.

A question occurred to him: how does the snake
swim so fast without any fins? He took out his spy-
glass and watched its movement through the water as

it reached the far side of the pool and slithered out. He mentally replayed the snake's peculiar looping motion as he had seen it in the water, and realized it had been making a combination of horizontal and vertical curves.

This gave him an idea. He went to look for his workers and found them cooking a meal in their hut. He asked them to eat quickly, then go to the sawmill and bring back three hundred larch slats. He then showed them how to nail these slats at a slanting angle into the base of the flume. Through the evening, the forest echoed with the sound of hammering.

Towards midnight, when he returned home, he found a message from the Chief Forestry Commissioner, telling him that the Prince, Princess and several experts would be along in the morning to observe the trial run. He hurried back to the site, an hour's walk away, and promised the workers three times their hourly rate of pay if they would work through the night and complete the job by 8 in the morning. In the event, they finished by 7.30. He sent them away for their breakfast, with offers of more incentives if they would agree to return to the sluice at 9.30.

The royal party arrived. His workers opened the sluice gate and started prodding the logs into the flume. A heavier log slipped in among the lighter ones, and the workers tried to move it discreetly out of the way. One member of the party saw this and shouted for it to be let through. Schauberger nodded his agreement. The log floated across the pool, and when it reached the flume intake it blocked the entrance, causing the water level to rise behind it. Everyone stared at the log. In a moment the flume would overflow.

There was a gurgling sound as the heavy log started to move. It swung to left and right, then shot down the flume. It sped along, snaking from side to side, and disappeared from sight around the curve. (see NAT, pp.52–53)

Later, Schauberger further developed the idea suggested by the water snake, of the slats in the logging flume. He used it in the device to help river regulation, so that it does not eat into its banks, and patented another to improve the flow in water pipes. Both these devices encourage the water to spiral inwards, so that the direction of movement is turned towards the centre of the spiralling motion, thereby relieving pressure on the banks or the pipe wall.

Egg-shapes are everywhere in Nature, once you start looking. The Earth's orbit around the Sun, usually described as elliptical, actually follows an egg-shape. Raindrops and flower-buds. If you look at a fish, such as a trout, it is egg-shaped in all three planes — seen from above, from the front, and from the side. A bird's body is egg-shaped. Art teachers suggest the egg-shape as the basis for drawing the human head.

A spiral fits comfortably into an egg-shape. When it grows narrower in width and correspondingly greater in intensity, it is moving towards the pointy end. If you store your eggs in the fridge with pointy end down, they will last longer. Amphorae, used by the ancients for storing food and drink, were in this otherwise impractical shape.

Schauberger says that an egg with the pointy end down is radiating outwards, whereas one with blunt end down is drawing into itself. The latter is the optimum shape for decomposition to occur. Consequently, he suggests that compost heaps should be in the shape of an egg with the blunt end down.

Every force ... unfolds itself and springs forth from the original form of life, the egg.

Viktor Schauberger, TFE, p. 8

Viktor Schauberger observes that egg-shapes have inherent buoyancy. This property helps the sap to rise in a tree. In daytime, the groundwater is drawn in via the roots, and towards the warmer crown of the tree. As the water warms, atmospheric oxygen mixes with the suspended carbon compounds, to form carbon dioxide. This carbon dioxide stays as egg-shaped bubbles in the capillaries. The buoyancy of these bubbles helps the sap to reach up to the crown of the tree.

He expresses his concern at plantation-style forestry practices, in which trees are exposed to more sunlight than they would naturally find. In an attempt to protect themselves from the extra heat, they grow more quickly. The capillaries are wider and more spongy, the carbon dioxide bubbles do not fit so snugly, the rising sap is not so nourishing, and the tree becomes diseased. Such practices, aiming for quantity of timber at the expense of quality, ultimately benefit no one, in his view.

One day before the official opening of the logging-flume, the chief forestry commissioner appeared on site. He forbade any further work, pending the arrival of an investigating commission. The commission, made up of local government and forestry administration officials, duly arrived. They surveyed the entire installation, and came to a dam, twenty yards high, enclosing a holding pool. They informed Viktor Schauberger that the dam was unsafe, and that It would not be strong enough to withstand the pressure of the incoming water, once the sluice gates were opened.

Schauberger said nothing in reply. He took his shotgun and walked down to the dam. He walked out on to the dam wall, and fired two shots into the air. If ever the officials had doubts about Herr Schauberger's mental stability, his behaviour now seemed to confirm their suspicions. However, unknown to them, two shots from his shotgun were the prearranged signal to his men to open the large sluice-gate higher up the flume.

They heard a roaring sound. Schauberger pointed upstream, to a rapidly approaching wall of water in which

logs and tufts of grass could be seen churning about in
a chaos of froth and water. The commissioners franti-
cally shouted and gesticulated to him to come to a place
of safety. Schauberger stayed put, and pretended to lean
down to examine the dam wall on which he was standing.
He had designed the basin in an egg-shape and was
confident that it would hold. The first rush of water
entered the basin, curved around, and turned its force
against the incoming water behind it. The logs stood up
and even leapt out into the air in the maelstrom, before
the entire basin was filled to its capacity of a million
cubic metres and water and logs all settled down. (see
NAT, pp.53–54)

Life is born from eggs. Where an egg-shape appears in
Nature, it is an embryo for the next incarnation, be it a bird, a
fish, or a finer form of energy. Every dewdrop holds the promise of new life. If it is a result of cooling, such as a flowerbud,
it gives birth to new life in a physical form. If it is the result of
warming, such as a dewdrop, it gives birth to energy, which we
feel as a tingling as we walk on the wet grass.

The Holy Grail — the extreme egg-shape (the calyx)

Viktor Schauberger

From water to air

Viktor Schauberger sees a trace, a progression, in the way different species lay their eggs. Fish, spending their lives in the
medium of water, lay shell-less eggs. The eggs are nourished
and protected by the water and its contents. Amphibians, who
are able to live in the medium of air, still have to protect their
eggs with a covering of water. Some newts, he says, lay their
eggs in moist holes, and then cover them with urine and a

secretion from their stomachs. Others lay eggs with a leathery skin. The problem is always that, out of the medium of water, the eggs must be protected from harmful influences, while being nourished with food of a sufficiently high quality.

Birds' eggs represent a further step in this progression. Their eggs are a masterpiece of engineering. The eggshell has to protect the new life inside, and allow food of the correct quality to filter through. It is a strong shape, and yet so fine as to allow the nourishing substances to diffuse through to the developing life inside. And among the most remarkable of these is the golden eagle, who lays its eggs at altitudes where the air is rarefied and the atmosphere is too thin to moderate the strength of the Sun's rays.

Schauberger believed that the Ancients applied the same principle to water conduits and burial chambers. The stones were treated in such a way as to allow a similar process of diffusion of nourishing energies, while protecting the contents from harmful influences. This allowed them to create artificial mountain springs with high quality water, rising to wooded groves. He says the conduits were made of natural stone pipes laid with mortar. The mortar was either sand and lime, or 'Roman mortar,' made with volcanic ash instead of sand.

He believed that similar systems can still be found in Mexico, in the form of pyramids and obelisks, whose outer surfaces have been treated to allow them to diffuse the air. The process was then facilitated by capping the buildings with golden roofs and spires.

Due to the presence of the necessary catalysts, they functioned like true eggshells. They therefore became veritable breathing mechanisms, enabling the various elements enclosed in the old masonry to be emancipated.

Viktor Schauberger, TFE, p.28

Untitled drawing by Viktor Schauberger

For Schauberger, such an application of the way Nature works is part of the human remit. As the animal kingdom has freed itself from the domain of water through refining the way the young are incubated, so a fully functioning human society gives expression to the same urge to elevate.

Ancient peoples, or rather their rulers and those who directed their lives (high priests), did exactly the same thing, for the true purpose of evolution is to raise everything to a higher level of development or unfoldment.

Viktor Schauberger, TFE, p.28

Schauberger believed that the technology of the egg-shape, and the spiralling movement which naturally fits within it, could be applied today. It could be adapted to provide high-quality water, both for drinking and for watering food crops. It holds the secret of new forms of energy, which could replace the petrol and diesel engines that he found so destructive, wasteful and dangerous. Thus humanity, freed from hunger, would finally be restored to health and have freedom of movement on land, under water and in the air.

Schauberger described mature, health-giving water, of the kind that emerges from a mountain spring, as ENNOBLED WATER. He patented an egg-shaped device to convert tap water into high-quality springwater. By means of the materials in the vessel, the flow that is encouraged and the correct temperature gradient, the water is able to reabsorb the necessary trace elements and re-energize itself. Schauberger tested such water on himself, and found it beneficial. Friends and acquaintances heard about it, and asked to try. There were stories of remarkable cures from chronic ailments in a matter of weeks. Kidney stones, rheumatism, malaria — all diminished after the sufferer drank some of the water from Schauberger's egg-shaped vessel. Even cancers went into decline. However, in Austria, the law was that only qualified medical doctors were permitted to cure people, and the authorities heard about it. It was deemed that his water was illegal, and he had to discontinue the investigation.

Viktor Schauberger tells a magical story from one of his expeditions in the forest. There was a high mountain valley, which many years previously, had been blocked off by a landslide. Since then, no one had visited it.

Using a rope and grappling hook, he climbed up to the valley entrance. He walked into undisturbed woodland, with old, tall spruce and larch trees and a healthy understorey growing beneath them. He saw wild mountain goats, chamois, which saw him too and were curious rather than afraid. This piqued his pride as a hunter. Although they were wary of him, they did not give their piping warning call.

As usual, his excuse for this trip was hunting. He was in pursuit of a wood-grouse. Walking further into the valley, he found the branch where it perched to sing its morning song, beside the clearing where it performed its displays. He looked for a place to wait. He found a suitable tree a short distance away, leant against it, wrapped his coat around himself to keep warm, and settled down to wait for the dawn. It was a moonless night. It grew so dark, there under the trees, that he could not see his hand in front of his face. He fell asleep.

When he awoke, it was still dark, but the darkness was illuminated by a small flame in front of him. It wasn't a fire, rather a reddish-coloured flame just above the ground. He had heard of will o' the wisp, and thought maybe this was one. He continued to watch it.

His attention was then caught by a luminous egg-shape, hovering over a mound in the clearing. This apparition was so strange that it brought him to his feet. It stayed suspended in the air above the small mound, with its pointed end down, emitting a yellowish glow. It grew larger, until it was about two yards high and a yard wide. By now, he was shaking with fear and cold.

He approached the glowing unearthly egg, his knees knocking together in his fright. It gave off no heat or smell. He put his hand into it, and felt nothing, saw no shadow. He noticed that the mound was covered with small white flowers. He lifted the turf underneath it with the end of his staff, but saw nothing. The egg continued to glow, undisturbed, giving off its colourless light.

He walked back to his tree, and stayed watching it. Eventually it began to fade and went out. Shortly afterwards, the air grew warmer and the dawn started to break.

He went back to look at the mound in daylight. There were delicate, beautiful white flowers all over the mound, with large dewdrops resting on their petals. When he touched one of the dewdrops, it fell heavily to the ground, as if it had been knocked off the flower by a hammer.

He prodded the mound with his staff, but found nothing unusual. Then his staff hit a resistance. It was a chamois horn. He investigated further, and found more horns, and finally the almost intact body of a chamois. The bullet that had presumably killed it was still there, in its foreleg. It was now long after the hunting season, so although it looked as if it had recently fallen, this animal must have been dead for some time. He realized he was standing on a chamois graveyard. He carefully put all the turf back, and left the valley.

What they called heaven is in reality a concentration similar to a fructigen-sac in a fertilized chicken's egg, which floats and slowly turns around its own axis under the influence of constantly-fluctuating variations in temperature. In the process, a gentle life-current will be emitted in the form of impulses which, with a moist tongue, can be sensed as a coolness at the pointed end of the egg and as a warmth at the rounder end. If the gyrations of this life-motor are increased through higher temperatures produced by a brooding hen or the brooding Sun, then in the protoplasm, enclosed by the coarse and fine material of the eggshell, a mysterious weaving and coiling about the yolk begins. A maternalistic expansion and an enveloping, loving and nurturing motion begins, which leads to the consumption of that substance in which has been instilled the irresistible urge so ardently awaited.

Viktor Schauberger, NAT, p.177

5. The Rhythms of Life

Viktor Schauberger knew that a mountain stream was colder the closer one came towards the source, and wondered if this had anything to do with the trout's ability to stay motionless in its fast-flowing water. He conducted an experiment, to test his theory of the significance of these small changes in temperature.

He selected a point on a stream where he had seen a motionless trout. He asked a group of his men to take a cauldron a few hundred yards upstream, fill it with water and light a fire under it. This they did. He returned to watch the trout. When the water was heated, the men poured it into the stream. Within a few moments the trout started flailing and thrashing about. Despite its strenuous efforts, it was unable to maintain its position and was carried away downstream. Some time later, it quietly returned to its original position.

This was a large, fast-flowing stream, so a single cauldron of warm water would not greatly affect the overall temperature. However, it was clearly significant to the trout.

The magical forest

Temperature is critical for the processes of life. A difference of part of a degree determines whether an egg will decompose or develop. It determines whether a seed will stay dormant or burst into new life.

If you walk in natural woodland, under the tall trees, you can hear the wind and see the sunlight in the treetops. But where you walk, on the forest floor, it is still and cool. As you tread on the soft leaf-litter, with the tree canopy far above your head, you are shielded from the excesses of the weather outside. Viktor Schauberger talks about how the mature trees regulate the microclimate beneath them, protecting their offspring so that they in turn can flourish.

> *With her fluttering leaves and waving branches, the mother-tree diffuses her oxygen and makes this now high-grade nutritive material available to young saplings beneath, which can only absorb it in this way.*
>
> *Viktor Schauberger, TFE, p.11*

Trees are long-lived. They are part of a complex ecosystem, containing and nourishing many lives. It is an environment which humans can destroy, but not easily create. Looking at the trees themselves, they are a marvel. The sap rises all the way up their straight trunks, to reach and feed the leaves far above, at their crowns.

The term BIOCENOSIS describes the collectivity of organisms within an area. Each living part of the biosphere, each plant and animal, makes its own contribution to the quality of the whole. Each adds its unique flavour to the groundwater, which enriches and sustains its companions. The trees, being long-lived, allow a complex ecosystem the time it needs to develop under their protection. For Viktor Schauberger, this was crucial to the health of all. This environment allows the higher forms of life to evolve. However, it is fragile. Reduction in biocenosis means that one or more of the contributors to this totality is not there to play its part. This leads to poorer quality groundwater, sick plants and animals and ultimately, sick humans.

With plantation monoculture, the trees struggle to obtain the nutrients they need from the water available. They become net consumers of water, taking in more water than they produce, thus eventually drying out the soil. In natural woodland with its wide diversity of life, the water is imbued with high-quality nutrients. Schauberger believed that this kind of woodland becomes a net producer of water. The trees are sustained by small quantities of water, leaving the water table high and the springs flowing.

He was horrified by the practice of clear-felling: cutting down all of the trees in an area, so that the ground is directly exposed to the Sun. This, in his view, overheats the ground. It causes the water table to sink, leading to drought and ultimately the death of the forest. This does not mean that no timber can ever be taken, however. Schauberger advocated selective felling: harvesting the mature trees so that their offspring can take their place and the collectivity of the forest can continue.

The forest is the habitat of water and as such the habitat of life processes too, whose quality declines as the organic development of the forest is disturbed.

Viktor Schauberger, TFE, p. 98

How sap rises

How does sap rise to the crown of a tall tree? Capillary action is part of the process. But anyone who has trailed the hem of their clothes in a puddle of water will know that capillary action has limited power. It draws water in the fabric of our clothes a few inches, not more. In a tree, too, mechanical capillary action cannot be the whole explanation. For a start, the sap has to rise, not fall. When a hedge-layer cuts a stem from the old hedge and lays it down, the stem must slant above the level of the cut. If the stem is lower than the level of the cut, then it will die. The sap has to go upwards, against gravity. Clearly, subtle processes are at play. In Schauberger's view, temperature also plays a part.

He observed the following phenomenon above stands of conifers. At about noon, on warm, still days, fine wraiths of mist can be seen rising from the tips of the trees, which disappear in

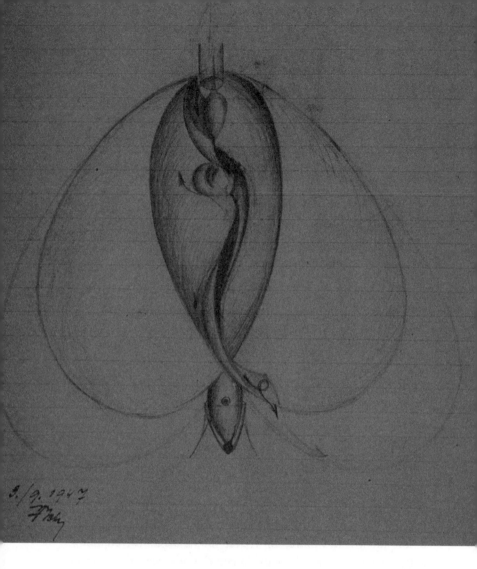

Untitled drawing by Viktor Schauberger

the light and heat. In his view, this is a consequence of a negative temperature gradient. The sap in the trees, containing valuable carbon compounds, is drawn rapidly upwards into the air, where it interacts with atmospheric oxygen. He says the old foresters used to watch out for this at lunchtime and pack a raincoat in their rucksacks when they saw it, as they knew it meant that it would rain in the afternoon. Such mist is not seen over mixed woodland, where the temperature is more constant.

Viktor Schauberger trained as a forest warden, not a plant biologist. He learned from what he saw around him in the forests and mountains. Some of his understandings correspond to what is written in botany textbooks; others do not. He was only marginally interested in the process of photosynthesis, for example. (The way that plants can use the green chlorophyll in their leaves to access sunlight energy in the daytime. They use this energy to break down water in the sap and combine it with atmospheric carbon dioxide, to form starches and other carbon compounds.) What interested him more was the way water is the medium for these interactions to happen, powered by its changing temperatures, alternating between night and day and through the seasons of the year.

In the daytime, there is a positive temperature gradient from the outside of the trunk to the inside, as the outside is warmer and the thick bark protects the inside. This temperature difference is uniform but small, moderated by the leaf canopy high above. The sap towards the outside of the trunk warms and expands, squeezing the cooler sap in the centre. As it is already buoyed up by the egg-shaped air bubbles, this also helps the sap to rise. Atmospheric oxygen, which he describes as 'male,' becomes more active in warm conditions, towards the sunny side of the trunk, while carbon compounds (for Schauberger, female substances) are more lively in cool conditions, towards the shady side. The marriage of these two leads to the procreation of more complicated compounds, such as starches and proteins. At night, the temperature gradient is reversed. Oxygen is released in the centre of the trunk, causing it to warm up, and the outside of the trunk is cooler.

For Viktor Schauberger, a tree's bark represents a similar feat of engineering design to an eggshell. Temperature is a form of radiation, one of the lower forms. The higher forms include sunlight energy, which can burn if one is not adequately protected. The bark offers this protection to the sensitive inner processes of the tree.

If we observe alders ranged along the banks of a stream, we can see that they do not grow towards the light, but arch towards each other, the tops of their crowns almost touching. They thus create a vault containing the right nutritive or diffusive mixture, which they then inhale through the bark, the latter's function being analogous to gills.

Viktor Schauberger, TFE, p.118

Trees vary in their ability to tolerate direct sunlight on their trunks. In line with conventional forestry, Viktor Schauberger divides them into LIGHT-DEMANDING and SHADE-DEMANDING varieties. Light-demanding trees, such as English oak, have thick bark, insulating them from the Sun. Shade-demanders, such as beech and pine, cannot cope with too much light and warmth directly hitting their trunks. It disrupts the temperature gradient, which governs the flow of sap to the crown. In woodland which has been left to itself, these trees grow tall with straight trunks. There is a thick canopy of branches, so that very little direct sunlight reaches the ground. In such woodland, the understorey is protected from the extremes of the weather outside.

Even one ray of sunlight is sufficient to alter the state of equilibrium between the body and the water.

Viktor Schauberger, TFE, p.55

If shade-demanders are planted in direct sunlight, they may grow branches all the way down the side of the trunk towards the Sun, or they swell their trunks with spongy growth. For

Viktor Schauberger, this second response is analogous to fever-ish swellings in animals and humans. In his view, the rapidly-grown, poor-quality timber produced by such forestry practices is the result of disease, not health.

He was very critical of this drive for quantity of timber at the expense of quality. Shade-demanding trees are over-exposed to sunlight, which causes disease, and plantation growth of single species deprives the forest of its biodiversity. One of the symptoms of ill-health in a living organism is an increase in temperature. Schauberger has shown how a rising temperature gradient, away from the anomaly point of four degrees Celsius, leads to expansion and decomposition.

Decomposition is part of the pulse of life, a necessary process to allow the next generation to form out of the remains of the previous one. To assist this breaking-down process, Nature calls on decay-inducing micro organisms, which proliferate in such conditions. Every living being has its own optimum temperature, where the internal flora and fauna are held in equilibrium. Problems arise when, with overheating, these micro organisms are summoned into an otherwise healthy being, be it tree, animal, plant or person.

Water plays the role of the untiring carrier of light, energy and heat. First and foremost, it is the carrier of all the substances that create and sustain life.

Viktor Schauberger, TFE, p. 97

The salt of the Earth

Salts are formed of a metal and an acid, and are soluble in water. For example, the chemical name for table salt is sodium chloride. It is a combination of the sodium, a metal, and the acid chlorine. Salts contain trace elements which are necessary for the health of the plants. Temperature governs how these nutrient salts rise from inside the Earth, to nourish the vegetation on the surface. Salt dissolves in warm water, and is precipitated out when the water cools. Deep in the Earth, the groundwater reaches high temperatures, and is able to absorb the different salts. As the water rises, it cools towards the anomaly point. As long as the layer at the anomaly point is within reach of the roots of the vegetation, then the deposited salts are accessible to the growing plants. Water that sinks from the surface is deficient in salts and rich in oxygen. It passes down past the stratum at the anomaly point. It sinks into the Earth where it is warmed, and in the process of breaking down into its components, it generates still more heat. Heat means expansion, and so it rises, and is now able to collect salts on its return journey.

For the salts to be available to the plants, the water table must be high. Anything that would cause the water table to sink, such as plantation monoculture or overheating of the surface by removal of the vegetation, will disrupt the process. This leads to less healthy plants and animals. Viktor Schauberger noticed the growth of trees which had received water deficient in these salts. Their lower trunks were sound, as the salts had reached this level, but higher up, towards the crown, they looked scrawny, as if they had been attacked by an animal.

Did the farmer but know how important the forest is, he would cherish it as he would life itself.

Viktor Schauberger, TFE, p.107

For him, the optimum profile of a healthy tree is a tall cylinder, with uniform width all the way up the trunk. It grows perpendicular to the ground, on a different plane from the Earth, as if extruded from the Earth itself. A conical shape, such as that of the classic Christmas tree, is a symptom of its inability to maintain a constant temperature gradient all the way up its trunk. The tree has been unable to carry the valuable carbon compounds very high, and so has deposited them lower down.

Viktor Schauberger felt that foresters could learn a lesson about woodland management from the way a cow grazes. The cow gathers a tuft of grass with her tongue, turns it around its own axis, and then pulls. This causes the grass stems to break at the right place. Not only that, the cow then nuzzles the grass with her wet mouth, which causes a change in the polarity in the air around the cut grass, allowing the wound to seal almost immediately. And finally, the weight of her body compacts the grass that has been loosened by her tugging, and in the process she returns more heat to the ground than was removed by the vacuum created by her tugging. This means that, despite the fact that the cow has taken some grass away, the process of doing so means that even more energy is returned to the Earth, so that the pasture can continue to increase in health, diversity and fertility.

He also observed the way traditional farmers cut the grass with a scythe. The scythe is hammered and sharpened in the evening. The following morning, before the Sun has risen high enough to shine on the field to be cut, the farmer scythes the dew-laden grass at a low cutting angle. The charge that has built up overnight in the scythe is insulated by the wooden handle, and so cauterizes the wounds in the grass. In this way, both field and cut fodder maintain their energies. Neither is wasted by being discharged into the atmosphere. As the Sun rises higher, the scything becomes more and more of a labour, no matter how keen the blade. The scythe loses its accumulated charge, the farmer stops scything for the day and stores it out of direct sunlight, so that it can charge up again.

He observed the same process in Nature on autumn mornings. At sunrise, when there is scarcely a breath of breeze, dead leaves flutter to the ground in their thousands. As soon as the Sun has risen enough to warm the air, this stops. For Schauberger, this early morning sunlight has the greatest intensity, and results in the greatest production of oxygen. The oxygen cauterizes the wound left by the separation of the leaf as it fell from the parent tree, and so the open wound is quickly sealed. (see TFE, pp.113–15)

6. Natural Magnetism

Some of the sights accorded to Viktor Schauberger are quite simply beyond the experience of most of us. Hearing about them, they seem utterly bizarre, almost unimaginable.

One such incident took place on an extremely cold winter's day. He was hunting mountain goats, chamois. He shot a buck, which toppled down into a ravine when it died. He scrambled down the bank after it. Fortunately, it had not broken through the ice as it fell on to the stream at the bottom of the gorge. He prepared the chamois' body to take it home.

Afterwards, he walked over the ice to a stretch of open water to wash his hands. He looked down into the cold, still, crystal-clear water. It was several metres deep. As he looked, he noticed several large logs moving below him, in a curious dance. The end of one log floated upwards, approaching another log. When it came near to the other log, it bounced back as if repelled, and settled down again. Then another log repeated the dance. Schauberger was fascinated. He forgot the chamois, and spent the rest of the afternoon stretched out on the ice, oblivious of the cold, watching the movement of these large, heavy beech logs down in the still, deep water.

As evening fell, it grew even colder. The full Moon began to rise. The logs' gyrations increased. Suddenly, one of them stood upright and shot straight up into the air. As it broke through the surface of the water, it was encircled with a necklace of ice. Other logs followed, and for a few minutes several of them silently performed their dance, each projecting just above the water, with a lacy collar of ice.

And more wonders were to follow! He looked down into the water once more, and saw further movement. Some large, egg-shaped stones on the floor of the stream started to move in the way the logs had done. They forgot that they were subject to the law of gravity, drifted towards each other and sprang away again.

As the full Moon rose higher in the sky, he now turned his attention to these stones. One stone, about the size and shape of a human head, began to gyrate in a more complete circle. Then it too rose to the surface, to be encircled with a collar of ice. Other stones joined it, and for a while, there in the cold moonlight, the patch of open water was speckled with stones, gently rocking in their mysterious dance.

With magnetism, like repels like. This, Viktor Schauberger believed, was what happened to the logs and stones in the pool. They were magnetized under the influence of the cold water and the light of the full Moon, and so they repelled each other.

A dynamo, such as that which powers a bicycle lamp, has three ingredients. These are movement (in the case of the bicycle, provided by the turning wheel), magnetism (a small magnet inside the dynamo) and electricity (which lights the lamp). If two are present, then the third will appear. With the bicycle lamp, magnetism and movement are present, so electricity is generated to light the lamp. Schauberger contends that while this is clearly true with technical motion (such as a dynamo), the same principle works with original motion. The difference is in the quality of magnetism and electricity. One leads to levity and growth, the other to weight and destruction. The dancing logs and stones rose to the surface because they became supercharged under the influence of BIOMAGNETISM in the moonlight and the cold water.

For everyday purposes, magnetism is what makes the piece of iron in a compass point north. However, there are at least three types of magnetism known to physics, and the one that is demonstrated in a piece of iron is called ferromagnetism ('ferro' means iron). Ferromagnetic materials have a north and south pole, and attract other ferromagnetic materials to align with them.

Viktor Schauberger was very interested in another type of magnetism, known as DIAMAGNETISM *(dia* meaning 'across' in Greek). Diamagnetism is the name for the field generated by the electrons spinning around the nucleus of an atom. All matter is composed of atoms, so every substance is residually diamagnetic. In the presence of a ferromagnet, these materials are deflected away, at right angles to the magnetic field.

Diamagnetic materials include carbon, copper, water, gold and silver. However, some materials are more susceptible to ferromagnetism, to the extent that their natural diamagnetism is overridden. Substances that do this are PARAMAGNETIC. Each atom in such materials lines up in the direction of the external ferromagnetic field, although they cannot hold any magnetism themselves. When they are moved away from the external ferromagnetic field, they revert to their original non-aligned state. Paramagnetic materials include oxygen and aluminium. The air is paramagnetic. So there is a difference between the electromagnetic properties of the water in the Earth and atmospheric oxygen.

It is estimated that the Earth contains four percent iron. This means that there is a weak ferromagnetic field over the whole of the Earth and extending into the atmosphere, where the paramagnetic atmosphere aligns with it. A magnetic compass needle lines up with this field when it points north. This field causes the diamagnetic materials in the Earth, such as the water and organic matter, to move at right angles to it: upwards, in other words. Schauberger believes that in the light of the full Moon, water becomes diamagnetically supercharged, enabling it to transport objects that would otherwise be heavier than it, such as the logs and stones that he saw that night.

As usual, Schauberger went further than conventional thinking. For him, diamagnetism is the result of the in-winding, cooling and condensing movement he described as cycloid-spiral space-curve motion. This is how planet Earth moves, and the fluids within it. A fluid that moves in this way results in negative pressure and a diamagnetic field. The electricity generated in such a field, which our bodies can register when we stand in natural woodland or beside a stream, is cool and constructive. In contrast, the hot, destructive electricity that lights our houses is generated by centrifugal motion.

Many of his contemporaries found Viktor Schauberger's ideas difficult to accept, including the assertion that rolling pebbles under water could emit sparks. One of his friends, a magazine editor, told him that this was one claim too far, if he wanted to be taken seriously by the scientific community. Schauberger laughed his big laugh and said, 'Sparks under water? Haven't you ever seen them? Then I'll show you right away. Come along!'

He filled a bucket with water and took it to a dark corner. Then he put two pebbles in the bucket and rubbed them together under the water. There were the sparks! Just as if iron and flint had been rubbed together in the light. For his friend, this was a fairy-tale experience, which he subsequently demonstrated to other doubters.

For Viktor Schauberger, this phenomenon was the origin of the legends of the Rheingold, which many had reported seeing glinting in the waters of the Rhine. The sparks are the result of the rubbing together of stones under water, stones with a metal content. He believes that this is another example of biomagnetism, as like poles repel each other (magnetic materials are BIPOLAR, that is, they have two poles, north and south). He says that the best way to produce this sparking effect is to collect a stone from the upper reaches of a mountain stream, and then break it in two, so that the two parts have the same magnetic property.

Everything around us responds to one or another form of magnetism, and so interacts with whatever it comes into contact with. This means that everything around us is undergoing change, quickly or slowly. Even stones are subject to this process of change. Nothing stays the same; all is in movement. As long as Earth, water and air are allowed to move planetarily, the way the wind blows and water spirals downstream, then energy will be generated. As we have seen, an egg-shape encourages original motion, so this also is a key ingredient in the process. In Viktor Schauberger's view, life itself is concentrated energy. This continual exchange and interaction sets the scene for organic life to flourish on the Earth.

In an intermixture of bipolar elements, every motion triggers reactive effects of an atomic and imperceptible nature.

Viktor Schauberger, TFE, p.3

For electrical energy to be generated, a magnetic field must be present. Substances originating from the air have a positive electrical charge, those from the Earth and Moon have a negative potential. This is most dramatically seen in lightning, which happens when the difference builds up locally to such an extent that it is forced to earth itself. Rainwater, which absorbs oxygen and so acquires a positive charge, is referred to as ANODE-WATER. Groundwater, which acquires a negative charge on its upward journey to the surface, is described as CATHODE-WATER. In other words, the Earth is a huge, stately, self-recharging, spiralling battery. In a battery, energy flows from the cathode to the anode; out from the Earth into the atmosphere. On a larger scale, the Moon is the cathode, the Sun the anode, and the Earth's water is the electrolyte: the medium which allows the process of energy exchange to occur.

What this means for the rivers

As we have seen, water can carry a charge. For Viktor Schauberger, this fact has huge significance. It determines whether a river flows quietly or eats into its banks, whether the surrounding land is fertile or barren, and whether a glass of water is tasty and refreshing or flat and insipid.

If a body of water is depleted of its charge, as will happen if it comes into contact with metallic iron or through heating, then it is depleted. In an attempt to replenish itself, it will draw in the energy from elsewhere. Viktor Schauberger believes that this is what happens when river water passes through an iron grille, or a hydro-electric turbine. The iron drains it of any charge. (Iron has the ability to cause sparks. Each spark represents a discharge, a draining of the energy held in the metal.) The centrifuges of the turbine disrupt and reverse its original (planetary) motion. Schauberger makes reference to the pitting that he observes on the hydroelectric turbine blades. This pitting is a consequence of technical motion, in his view. With what he called 'original motion,' oxygen is held in suspension by the water. Technical motion prevents the water from carrying oxygen in suspension, so it is released. In this state oxygen is unstable and it eats into whatever it encounters, including the turbine blades. He objected to hydro-electric turbines for another reason. They disrupt the natural flow of the water in its in-winding, cycloid-spiral space-curve. They break up the structure of the water, with layers of progressively-warmer water spiralling around the cool core water-body.

After passing through the turbine the water attempts to recover its equilibrium and return to original motion: an in-winding motion. As it has been depleted of any charge it was carrying, it now replenishes itself. It draws in the charge that is present in the groundwater, leaving less to nourish the vegetation in the surrounding land. All that is needed to rectify this,

Drawing by Viktor Schauberger ➤

Luftabladung

m Nachschubkraft

zuerhalten.

is to stop doing what is damaging the water. A watercourse that flows the way it wants, at the temperature it wants, is nourishing to the life around it.

... survival or extinction is dependent on the regulation of electromagnetic interactions.

Viktor Schauberger, TFE, p.10

Similarly, a glass of flat, distilled water will draw into itself from the body of the person who has drunk it. It is known that drinking distilled water can be harmful, as it causes minerals to leach out of the body. In effect, the drinker nourishes the drink. A glass of fresh springwater, on the other hand, nourishes the drinker.

He proposed a novel design for a hydro-electric turbine. The water falls through a funnel, which has been rifled with spirals on its inside to encourage its natural in-winding motion. As it issues from the nozzle, the stream of water falls on to some corkscrew-like blades, which spin as a result of the impact of the high-speed falling water. With such a device, the water rotates around its own axis and so is not damaged in the process.

7. How Things Grow

When he was a young forest warden, there was a farmer whom Viktor Schauberger sometimes visited. This man's farm had consistently healthy crops and high yields, but he was considered crazy by his neighbours, because he did everything in a different way and at different times from them.

One evening, at dusk, Viktor Schauberger called by. He found the farmer in a barn behind the farmhouse, standing in front of a large wooden barrel and singing a curious song into it. He had a large wooden paddle in his hand, and was stirring the contents of the barrel. The song was a sort of rising and descending scale, almost shouting. As the tone rose, he stirred in one direction. As his tone changed, he reversed the direction of stirring. From time to time, he stopped and took a handful of clay, which he crumbled and threw into the barrel, then continued stirring and singing.

Schauberger came closer, to have a look at the contents of the barrel. It was clear water. The farmer noticed him, smiled a greeting and continued the stirring and his strange song. Eventually, he took out the paddle and said, 'There, now it can ferment.'

Over a glass of cider in the farmhouse, the farmer explained what he had been doing. The clay contained aluminium. It was mixed into the cooling water, along with exhaled carbon dioxide as he sang into the barrel. This imbued the water with a neutral charge. After harrowing the fields with a wooden harrow, the charged water was sprinkled over them with fronds, like a blessing. The water evaporated, leaving crystals behind. The crystals permit the formation of a shimmering, high-quality violet net between the Earth and the sky. The old

farmer referred to this net as the 'hymen.' It enabled the
soil to stay moist and fruitful, even in the hot times of
the year.

The mixing of heaven and earth

In this chapter we look at Viktor Schauberger's understandings
of how things grow. In his view, physical growth is the result of
the marriage of two different kinds of energy, one kind incoming from the Sun and the other spiralling from inside the Earth
up to the surface. Schauberger refers to these kinds of energies
as ETHERICITIES. It is the interaction of these that allows life to
flourish on Earth.

He coined three new words, to help explain his perception
of how things grow: OXYGENE, CARBONE and FRUCTIGEN.

OXYGENE refers to the element oxygen, and more. It focuses
on its energetic properties. It is an ethericity caused by the
action of the Sun.

CARBONE refers to the element carbon, and all of its compounds. Carbones constitute the physical form of all of life on
Earth, from viruses to elephants.

FRUCTIGEN is the first Earth ethericity that we will meet
(two more will follow later). It is the energy associated with
carbones. It is released from the physical remains of life on
Earth, as they break down in the soil.

Oxygenes

Sunlight continually streams on to the Earth, and in the process it stimulates atmospheric oxygen. With light and warmth,
the oxygen becomes more active. In fact, Viktor Schauberger
goes further than this. He says that sunlight comes into existence as it meets the atmosphere. As it is dark between the
Earth and the Sun, maybe he has a point. Oxygen, which he

Untitled drawing by Viktor Schauberger

describes as the waste product of the Sun, is solidified sun-light energy.

Water, falling from the sky as rain, absorbs some oxygen, and in the process acquires a positive charge. We now take our first step into organic chemistry, Schauberger-style. He wants to distinguish between the element oxygen as described in chemistry textbooks, and the living, interacting energy form that he sees around him. Accordingly, he describes ethericities with this positive, masculine quality as OXYGENES.

Oxygenes are active when hot. In a forest, sunlight reaches through the leaves to the floor. The oxygen can then be proc-essed by the undergrowth, which may otherwise be burned. This process can be seen in dense woodland. The branches of the mother-trees pre-masticate the food in the sunlight for the saplings growing under their protection. Similarly, as the river rolls over the stones on its bed, small eddies are created. These eddies are orifices, which can take in atmospheric oxygen.

Carbones and fructigens

The element carbon is the basis of the molecules that form the bodies of all life on Earth, from viruses to plants to insects to elephants. As Viktor Schauberger is interested in a slightly different process, he gives a slightly different name to all of these building-blocks of life. His term for them can be translated as CARBONES. When any vegetation dies down, it is either converted back into the growth medium for further growth, as humus, or it is stored in the earth itself, as coal, oil or gas. The energy potential in this store of carbon compounds is referred to as FRUCTIGEN. Schauberger stresses the fact of its sweet, fatty, emulsifying nature, in contrast to the acidic quality of oxygenes.

Fossil fuels thus represent an energy bank for the Earth, the deposit account for future fructigens. The groundwater rises through this material on its way to the surface, and absorbs some of the fructigen. He says that the plants are equipped to take in the accumulated charge from the groundwater via little nodes on their roots, which he named as ROOT-PROTOPLASMS. The groundwater rhythmically discharges its accumulated energy into these little egg-like sacs. This is part of the pulse of the Earth, as felt by the vegetation. These sacs are very delicate, and collapse when the plant is uprooted and they are exposed to the air. The plant has to create them anew after it has been transplanted.

Around high mountain springs, nourishing herbs grow. Viktor Schauberger often found sick and wounded animals there, grazing these plants. Eating them seemed to

help the healing process. Water at these springs is low
in dissolved oxygen and high in trace elements and carbon compounds. He believed that the high quality of
the springwater that has nourished these plants enables
the plants in their turn to heal the mountain animals.
It also enables the animals to heal the damaging effect
of the Sun's rays on their skin in the thin mountain air.
Denied access to these places, he believed, the highly-
charged sunlight would burn their skin and the animals
would become mangy. The old foresters told him, with a
wink and a smile, that drinking the water of such springs
helped them to stay virile to a ripe old age.

*This upwelling flow was called healing water by the old
huntsmen, because it alleviated gout, arthritis and other
ailments of old age. Smirking, they declared emphatically
that it restored virility or maintained it right into old
age, which was why even feudal lords, who had become
slightly doddery, never failed to drink the water from
these youth-restoring springs.*

Viktor Schauberger, TFE, p.30

The interaction between oxygenes and fructigens

Oxygenes penetrate the atmosphere on the vertical plane. The
fructigens spiral upwards through the Earth in the groundwater.
Carbon-based vegetative growth is the result of the marriage
of atmospheric oxygen, charged by the Sun, and these fructigens. They meet where plants grow at the surface of the Earth.
Schauberger names this zone the GEOSPHERE. The geosphere is
electrically neutral.

In Schauberger's description, JUVENILE WATER is the by-
product of the cool interaction between these two ethericities,
oxygenes and fructigens. It is not ready to drink yet. It has to

go through the cycle of maturation by sinking into the Earth and rising again, to acquire salts and more fructigens. Then, when it emerges at a spring, it is ripe enough to nourish plants and animals.

Water is an organic magnet, and at the same time a transformer, a receiver and a transmitter. It is the mediator or accumulator of growth, which mediates life ...

Viktor Schauberger, WW, p.55 footnote

Oxygenes are more active the warmer they are, whereas fructigens become more potent in cool, dark conditions. Viktor Schauberger points out that in the engine of a diesel car, there is also a reaction between oxygen and carbon compounds. However, this is a centrifugal reaction, which happens under heat and pressure. It results in a lot of noise, the destruction of the components, some energy and some toxic waste products. He also points out that from an energy perspective, it is inefficient. He contrasts this with the cool, moist, silent, constructive process of vegetative growth, tempered by the cooling effect of the wind through the trees.

The element hydrogen also plays a part in his system. He sees hydrogen as the ultimate carrier medium for all of the processes described here. Carbon and hydrogen form the building blocks of living things. The science of organic chemistry is devoted to their study. The chemical definition of water is a molecule consisting of two hydrogen atoms and one oxygen atom.

Taken separately, and subjected to heat and pressure, oxygen and hydrogen will explode and burn. When the circumstances are right, however, it is Schauberger's contention that the hydrogen can bind the otherwise aggressive oxygen, to form water. Heat and pressure produce fire; cool and a biological vacuum lead to water and carbon-based vegetative growth.

Both warming and cooling are part of a cycle, like day and night, an alternating rhythm in the processes of growth. When fructigens are more potent, under cool conditions, the interaction happens in the medium of water, and is constructive. Under a falling temperature gradient, towards the anomaly point of four degrees Celsius, the fructigens, assisted by hydrogen, are able to bind the oxygenes. This leads to the formation of carbon compounds — in other words, physical growth — and water.

For Schauberger, this meeting of positive and negative energy is the process of prime importance in the geosphere. It is the union of masculine and feminine life-energies on a solar-system scale, and it leads to the birth of the next generation on planet Earth. As we have seen, the movement of a body of water in its course mimics the movement of the planet through the heavens. In the same way, every time the female of a species invites a male to pair up and produce the next generation, they are participating on a small scale in the marriage between Earth and Sun energies that is happening around us all the time.

As always, problems arise from human interference. Organisms that are designed for cooling processes will be damaged if heat, light and oxygen are introduced. In the forest, the mother-trees filter the sunlight for their saplings. In the same way, our lungs condition the oxygen we breathe in, so that it can be bound by the fructigens carried in our blood, which themselves have been filtered by the intestines.

The cycle of physical life

For growth to occur, decay must have already happened. Viktor Schauberger is interested in this transformation, the breakdown of an organism into simpler components. In particular, he looks at the different processes of fermentation. In wine-making, the yeast goes through two initial stages. In the first stage the yeast organism breathes in oxygen, eats the fruit pulp, breaking it down into fruit juice, and exhales carbon dioxide. This allows the yeast to multiply. In the second stage, light and oxygen are excluded and the yeast goes into a different process. It eats the complex fruit sugars, and in so doing breaks them down into alcohol, which is a simpler carbon compound. In both stages, it breathes out carbon dioxide and energy is released.

Viktor Schauberger is particularly interested in this second process of COLD FERMENTATION which, he believes, allows higher qualities of energy to be emitted. It is his contention that the difference between these two processes was well known in certain circles. It is why the bodies of important people were often buried in coffins of specific metals in a cool vault, from which heat, light and oxygen-rich rainwater were excluded. When bodies are allowed to slowly decompose in this way, an eerie light can sometimes be seen nearby on dark nights. The energy associated with this process emitted the cold light that he once saw on a moonless night above the chamois' grave.

This is why, as a particularly sly old forester explained, the high clergymen had themselves buried in a constantly cool church crypt, or why the more common priests at least had a little roof built over their graves along the cemetery wall at the eastern side in order to protect them from rainwater.

Viktor Schauberger, NAT, p. 94

Everything that dies eventually returns its remains to the Earth. The ancestors of the vegetation that is alive now have died and decayed, leaving their remains in the soil. Through decay and cold fermentation, the organization that once was a tree is broken down into a mass of vegetable matter. The groundwater passes through these remains on its journey to the surface, as it is drawn to meet the incoming solar energy. As it comes into contact with them, it is imbued with fructigen, the essential quality of living things, embodied in the complex carbon compounds that were formed during the ancestral plants' own processes of life and growth. This allows the next generation of living things to condense and have process.

Applying these ideas to agriculture

In his later years, Viktor Schauberger turned his attention to agriculture. He designed two devices to stimulate the process of cold fermentation of vegetable matter or animal manure, which when spread over the land, would foster the formation of the 'hymen' that the old farmer had talked about many years earlier.

The first is for animal manure. Dig an egg-shaped chamber in the ground. Make sure that the sides are sealed enough to be watertight, and that it is insulated from external light and heat. Fill the chamber with fresh finely-chopped stable manure and liquid manure. Then top it up with water with a high volume of dissolved oxygen, such as rainwater, or river water that has been exposed to sunlight. Then add minerals of different potential, such as the aluminium-bearing clay sprinkled by the old farmer into his barrel of water. The cover of the chamber has a small motor in its centre, which powers a paddle to induce a vortex in the lower third of the chamber. The paddle itself preferably contains copper and zinc. At nightfall the cover is placed over the top of the chamber, to seal it from the air, and the motor is switched on. The following day there is no trace of any manure left in the chamber. It contains only sweet-smelling, energized water. In the evening small quantities of this exalted liquid manure are spread over the ground.

When the Sun shines on the soil the next day, the substances of Heaven and Earth can meet and mix, as Schauberger quotes from one of his favourite references, the Emerald Tablet of Hermes Trismegistus. As long as the resulting layer is not damaged by iron ploughs, Schauberger believed that this manure could lead to a nine-fold increase in productivity and return the deserts to cultivation.

The second of his ideas is a new take on an old tradition — that of compost-making. Select a tree, ideally a mature fruit tree with a broad leaf canopy. Dig a hole around the base of its trunk, taking care not to damage the roots. Protect the lower trunk with paper, bark or cardboard, up to the level of its first branches. Then put freshly cut grass, potato peel and other vegetable matter into the dug hole. Leaves and straw of crops already grown can also be added. Then sprinkle some powdered copper and zinc, a little salt and even smaller quantities of raw sugar on top of the mixture. Tread it in, and cover it with a layer of earth. The earth can be mixed with sand or gravel from a nearby stream. Repeat these layers as often as vegetable matter becomes available, gradually reducing the radius and piling it up against the cardboard around the tree trunk, so that the eventual heap has an egg-shape. When it is a complete egg-shape, seal off the air hole at the top with some leaves, and flatten the outside of it with the back of a shovel.

The first stage of fermentation happens in the summer, as the heap is built up and earthworms proliferate. In the autumn, the structure is sealed and covered with fallen leaves from the tree above it. In winter, the process of cold fermentation can take place in this sealed chamber. The following spring, the compost heap will bloom. This is a sign that it is ready. Spread the compost over the land with a copper or bronze shovel, and plough it in quickly. As a bonus, the fruit tree will produce a bumper crop the following autumn.

Heating and cooling processes alternate and pulsate through the whole of life. Where there is heat, expansion occurs, and so bacteria proliferate as a necessary part of this procession of breaking down what is no longer needed, so that it is available for the next generation. Schauberger sometimes refers to planet Earth as a dung-heap. Given that decay is a necessary part of the processes of life, we can begin to understand that he does so with respect for the complexity and interdependency of it all.

He believed that misuse of the Earth's stores of fructigen for techno-academic motion would destabilize the planet's weather systems. Already in the nineteen-thirties, he predicted that this would lead to storms, floods and other unpredictable weather patterns, as Mother Nature tries to adjust. Her energy banks are being appropriated for purposes which run counter to her natural way of progression. Life, in his view, is a movement towards ever-more complex, higher-grade substances. A reversal of that process is the way of death.

Growth is the direct result of the transmission of Will, which takes place through the rhythmical reversal in the polarity of the mediator of life, water.

Viktor Schauberger, TFE, p.162

Growth and decay are two parts of the same process, as a magnet has a north and south pole. Together they lead to evolution. For Schauberger, it is a given that evolution itself is an unfolding, refining process. As planet Earth is drawn through the heavens, so living things are drawn onwards. The ancestors appeared earlier in time, and so, in his view, they are less evolved than the current, appearing generation. The rising generation grows on the experience of those who have been this way before. The younger generation comes later, and so is evolutionarily older. This, in his view, applies equally to plants, animals and human beings. This means that all of life is predisposed to evolve and refine, and when the two processes of growth and decay are in the correct balance, this is what happens.

On his travels, Viktor Schauberger visited the monastery of Arles-sur-Tech in the eastern Pyrenees. This monastery has a crypt containing a large marble sarcophagus completely sealed from the air, and with a copper pipe

protruding from it, from which issues water with marvellous health-giving properties. It has been doing so for
at least seven hundred years. He tells how the monks
considered the healing properties of the water such a
mystery that they offered a reward for its explanation.
For Viktor Schauberger, the high quality of the water
was not a mystery. Every spring that gushes out of the
sarcophagus of the Earth and is protected from the sun's
rays has the potential for the same health-giving properties. In the crypt underneath this Pyrenean monastery
the preconditions were met. It is cool and dark. The
water is hermetically sealed in its marble vault, so that
no oxygen can reach it. And the copper pipe is the final
component, assisting the flow of life-enhancing energy in
the mature water as it issues out from the Earth.

*The source of life comes into being when the ethericities
of Earth bind those of Heaven. For this the maternal
forces and energies must be more powerful than the incident fertilizing substances, for if the process takes place
in reverse order, then fire is created.*

Viktor Schauberger, NAT, p. 98

8. Life Energies

After the success of his first logging flume, Viktor Schauberger went on to build other flumes over central Europe. At one of these installations, he designed a new kind of sluice gate, which encouraged the water to twist around itself like the stream of urine from a running wild animal. This flow allowed a central funnel to form, a shimmering vortex of energy moving in the opposite direction to the flow of water.

On the day of testing the new gate it was pouring with rain. He lay down, looking down into the vortex formed at the sluice gate. The rainwater dripped continuously from the brim of his hat, in front of his eyes. It did not fall straight into the funnel that he could see directly below him. The shiny cord of light in the centre of the spiral seemed to prevent it. Each drop from his hat was forced sideways, delineating a cone formation sitting on top of the funnel.

But not for long. Suddenly a jet of cold water erupted upwards and hit him in the face. He put this phenomenon down to the fact that the air was colder than the water, and so the funnel could not expand upwards. Instead, it expanded sideways, and as the cone broadened, pushed the water falling from his hat further to the side. The strengthening vortex caused more water to be sucked upwards and into his face, which was directly above it.

In this chapter, we look at the two other Earth ethericities described by Viktor Schauberger. They both result from original motion, an in-winding, concentrating, spiralling movement, which is seen in the progression of the planet through the heavens and the blood pulsing through our arteries and veins.

Untitled drawing by Viktor Schauberger

QUALIGENS radiate outwards, in a field surrounding the spiral-ling object, whether it is water flowing in a river or planet Earth moving in its course. DYNAGENS concentrate inwards, towards the centre of the spiral. We also look at one of the inventions he developed, which is a direct result of his understandings of these energies.

As we have seen, the cool marriage of oxygenes and fruc-tigens results in the growth of living things. Their interaction gives us our physical bodies, our first home. However, our bodies and those of all the plants and animals around us are only on short-term loan. They too will return to the soil in their time, to make way for the following generation. This cycle of growth and return is the first requirement for life to exist on Earth. Viktor Schauberger describes the carbones deposited for physical growth as ballast, discarded to allow higher energies to have process. Qualigens and dynagens are these related, longer-term energies.

All movement radiates energy. There is a different qual-ity of radiation associated with original and technical motion. Technical motion is the process Nature uses to break things down into their component parts. It is the motion of destruc-tion. It is difficult for creativity to occur within its field. To take an extreme example, it is not easy to think very deeply near noisy machinery. Musical sounds, also, can be enhancing or destructive: stimulating or preventing a thought process. Qualigens and dynagens have different effects when they are the result of technical motion.

Qualigen

Viktor Schauberger refers to the kind of energy radiated out-wards as qualigen, because it affects the quality of life for all who are touched by it. These forms of radiation affect the qual-ity of processes for all living things, including our own thoughts. Qualigens associated with original motion have an enhancing property. They come into existence as the result of the motion of creation. That is why it is refreshing and stimulating to take a walk in the wild places, in the forests and mountains and by the sea. In these places, away from the noise and radiation of machines, we can register the radiation of the life of the Earth. It is particularly noticeable at dawn and dusk, when the Sun is not dominant. Qualigens affect the quality of human thought processes, as well as our physical and mental health.

Qualigens affect the quality of vegetative growth, too. The radiated qualigens are absorbed by the groundwater, which in turn nourishes the vegetation. A healthy, lush vegetation keeps the land cool, allowing the groundwater to rise and nourish it, and so the cycle of life continues.

The planets, in their spiralling movement through the heavens, also radiate qualigens. Qualigens have a levitating quality. Viktor Schauberger talks about how young, healthy children and animals are so imbued with qualigens that they do not feel their own physical weight. Watching young children, one can see that this makes it difficult for them to stay still.

Planet Earth radiates them, and so does the Moon. It is known that the Moon exerts a pull on all of the water on the Earth; every day, it lifts the Pacific Ocean by a few metres. Changes in lunar gravity can be measured in a teacup, and tides are at their strongest at the time of full and new Moon. Traditionally, Austrian foresters transported the heaviest logs from the high mountains down the streams by the light of the full Moon, when the water was at its most buoyant. Sunlight, Viktor Schauberger's father told him, makes the water curl up and go lazy.

... the colossal carrying and tractive forces that maintain the whole earth in an unstable floating state and cause it to rotate in peculiar spiral space-curves (cycloid space-curve motion). They are the same forces that enable

everything that crawls and flies on this dung-heap —
Earth — to overcome their own physical weight.

Viktor Schauberger, EE, p.44

Dynagens

The third type of Earth ethericity, completing the trio with fructigens and qualigens, is also a consequence of original motion. Whereas qualigens radiate outwards, this energy flows in the opposite direction to the pull of gravity, upwards towards the centre of the spiral. Viktor Schauberger describes this kind of Earth energy as dynagen. It is dramatically displayed in the central updraft of a waterspout, where the vortex works in the opposite direction to the flow of water. In the same way, as the Earth is drawn onwards through the heavens in its spinning and spiralling dance, dynagen energy is drawn in towards it.

The Earth rotates in spiral space-curves about its diamagnetic axis. This axis is no axle, but a negatively potentiated concentration of dynagen, which arises through this inwinding motion. The axis itself is something akin to a hole into which seminal substances are sucked.

Viktor Schauberger EE, p.156

In Viktor Schauberger's view, this is the energy that the trout uses to stay motionless in the strong current of a mountain stream, and dart upstream like lightning when disturbed. There is a spiralling motion of the entire body of water, around the cooler core water-body. This causes dynagen energy to be generated, flowing in the opposite direction. The trout sits in this stream, adjusting its position as necessary with gentle movements of its gills, fins and tail. Heavy logs, floating just below the surface of the stream, are supported and braked by this energy.

For Schauberger, all that we see is in process, and that process is one of refinement and evolution, towards ever-increasing complexity. In the same way that oxygenes are concentrated sunlight, he tells us that dynagens are the energy counterpart of metals, the most refined physical elements naturally occurring on Earth.

Schauberger goes even further than this. He declares that under the correct conditions and with a falling temperature gradient, the metals contained in the stones will actually grow, in the process of solidification of bipolar dynagens. He tells us that this phenomenon was confirmed by the forensic scientist, Dr Zuckerkandl (see EE, p.23). He explains this by means of the effects of the two types of motion. Technical motion, in the presence of a rising temperature gradient, leads to expansion. Original (or planetary) motion, on the other hand, leads to concentration. When the conditions are right, the dynagen energy can solidify into its physical counterpart, metal.

He gives an example of this process in a flowing watercourse. As the stones carried in the stream are ground down by friction, heat is generated. The cooler water, approaching the anomaly point of four degrees Celsius, absorbs this heat from the surrounding, warmer water. The core water-body is also able to carry stones, pebbles and sediment downstream, where they will continue the process of abrasion. Metals contained in the stones are charged by this continual rubbing. This dynagen energy eventually concentrates into metals, which can be seen sometimes, glinting on the riverbed.

Every acid is a liquid metal, and without metal there is no energy or life-electricity of any kind.

Viktor Schauberger, TFE, p.176

Metals combine with other elements to form salts. Salts are soluble in water. They are present in urine and faecal matter, which has passed through an animal. These, then, are a source of concentrated dynagen. Viktor Schauberger says that the bladder would be a vacuum, making it impossible to pass water, were it not for the dynagen energy going in the opposite direction, allowing the urine to be expelled. This waste-matter can then encourage the further development of fructigen. Traditional gardeners know that urine is a very effective compost activator, speeding up the process of converting waste vegetable matter into fertilizer for the next generation of plants.

Once, Viktor Schauberger was invited to present his ideas about river regulation to a group of academics. This was in Austria in the nineteen-thirties, a time and place where status and qualifications were highly respected. Schauberger, with no training beyond that of a forest warden, was to address a group of University professors, including several hydraulic engineers. As he had been writing that they had got it all wrong, they were not predisposed to be sympathetic to him.

The Rector opened the discussion, asking him to summarize his ideas of natural river regulation, so that there is no erosion or water damage, leading to beneficial effects through the whole evolutionary chain. Schauberger replied that such concepts were not easily encapsulated in a few words. 'Come now,' said the Rector, 'perhaps you can highlight the essence of the matter with a few short phrases. Please keep it as brief and to the point as possible.'

To which Schauberger slowly and carefully replied: 'In the same way that a running wild boar passes water.' While factually accurate, this reference was almost certainly outside the Rector's experience, and it did not endear this upstart forester to him. Fortunately, the academic who had sponsored the meeting could see what

Schauberger was getting at. This gentleman was able to present the concept of original motion and its associated energies in more accessible language to his colleagues, and a lively, productive discussion ensued.

Viktor Schauberger believed that dewdrops embody the fertilization of negatively-charged dynagen by its atmospheric counterpart. As dynagens are associated with metals, this is more likely to occur where the soil is rich in trace elements.

The three ethericities, fructigens, qualigens and dynagens, also exist in association with outward-spiralling, technical motion, but there they have the opposite effect. So dynagens resulting from centrifugal motion lead to decomposition: the destruction of life. With original motion they lead to an enhancement of vitality. Both are part of the pulsating rhythm of life, but for evolution and progression to occur on planet Earth, the balance must favour original motion.

Life itself ... is the highest conceivable concentration of dynagen

Viktor Schauberger

The three Earth ethericities described here form a hierarchy. Fructigens, the energy aspect of carbones, enter into union with oxygenes. They give birth to water and vegetation. He also describes fructigens as the embryos of qualigen. Physical carbon-based growth can be seen as the ballast, which is discarded when the qualigens are released. Qualigens, which have their life and expression through original motion, are so named because they govern the quality of process for all living things, including ourselves. The radiated qualigens allow life to flourish in all its variety, which sets the scene for the continuation of the process. At the same time as the qualigens, original motion causes dynagens to come into

existence. Dynagens, the highest and most potent of the three
ethericities, both allow life to be enhanced and set the conditions for the next generations of fructigens to form.
Problems occur when either original or technical motion
goes out of balance. And in Viktor Schauberger's opinion, this
is invariably a result of human interference. He alludes to the
catastrophe of Atlantis, for which he has a novel explanation.
He suggests that the Atlanteans were highly competent at harnessing levitational growth energies, and they eventually went
too far. They applied this technology so successfully that whole
sections of the Earth were torn out and lifted skywards, including the island of Atlantis itself.

*The high priests of ancient cultures had a command-
ing knowledge of this power, which they cherished and
guarded like life itself so as to be venerated as Gods for
their skill.*

Viktor Schauberger, EE, p.26

Nowadays, we are experiencing the opposite problem. Our
industry, our world is dependent on the decay-inducing processes of technical motion. An excess of destructive energy is
generated, which has a different set of consequences.

The perpetual motion machine

Viktor Schauberger's insights into these natural energies,
developed over years of observation in the forests and mountains, led on to ideas about how they could be used in machines.
He saw ways to use the energy associated with original rather
than technical motion. If successful, this would mean that the
machines would not issue poisonous waste and would not
destroy their fuel. The holy grail of perpetual motion would be

available to all. He tried many times to describe the moment when this panorama of possibilities, a way out of humanity's difficulties, was suddenly clear to him. He often made reference to the moment when he was standing beside the mountain stream and disturbed the trout, causing it to dart upstream against the current, and the sudden understandings that came to him there.

Thus it was that one day I came to understand the 'hereafter.' It is the great vault arching above us that a famous poet once called the 'Living Breath of God,' which is no empty phrase. Its significance will only become clear to those who know how to free the immense energies, material and immaterial, that are contained in every drop of water and in the smallest current of air.

Viktor Schauberger, NAT, p. 62

He made several attempts to develop machines powered by dynagen energy. Perhaps the most famous was developed in the late nineteen-thirties and early forties. It can work with water or air. It looks like a small flying saucer: a circular disc with a slightly raised centre. Surrounding the cup are two circular horizontal plates, one above the other. The plates have the shape of concentric waves, similar to those that form around the point where a pebble is thrown into a pond. On the side of each wave facing the centre there are slits like a fish's gills. A small conventional motor sets the plates into rotation around the spindle of the central cup. In the water-powered version, this draws the water into the cup, and disperses it outwards by technical motion. As with a trout's gills, the outward flow

Drawing for patent 146141, suction turbine or 'repulsine' ➤

P.A. 146141 * -4.3.40

abb.1

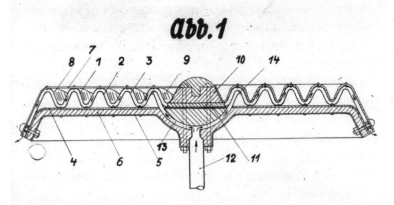

abb.2

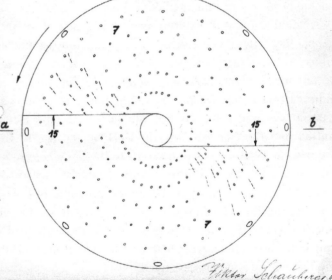

P.A. 146141 * -4.3.40

1.3.40

Viktor Schauberger in Wien-Haderadorf

Verfahren und Vorrichtung zur atomaren Umwandlung tropfbar
flüssiger oder gasförmiger Stoffe.

pushes the water through the slits. Then it falls into the space between the two plates and down the other side of the wave, drawing more in behind it. This process continues between and through each of the waves in the plate, until the water reaches the outer edge.

Once there it is directed towards one of several nozzles. These nozzles have the shape of a downward-pointing egg, with a central spindle designed to cause the fluid to wind in on itself. As it passes through the nozzles it falls and spirals inwards, creating vortices of dynagen energy in the opposite direction. The water then falls into a holding container, and is drawn back up through the central cone to repeat the process. As it moves through and out of the turbine, the water is enhanced in quality as well as producing power. The energized fluid can be drawn off. The resulting power can be used to generate energy or propulsion or to improve the quality of drinking water.

A small amount of external energy is required to start it off, but thereafter it is in essence a perpetual motion machine. Viktor Schauberger believed that such a device could be 98 percent efficient, compared to about 12 percent for conventional machines. He patented this device in 1940, when Austria was under the control of Nazi Germany. He was drafted into the German army in 1941, at the age of fifty-five, and in 1943 he was transferred to the SS. There he was obliged to continue this project, with the assistance of some concentration camp inmates. Using the principle of the suction turbine, they developed a levitation machine. The first time it was powered up, it rose silently to the ceiling of the hangar, trailing a blue-green and then a silver glow. It crashed into the ceiling and was destroyed.

Whether the project continued after that time has been the subject of much speculation. There are isolated stories and rumours, but the facts are elusive. It has been reported that at the end of the war, the Russian troops cleared all of the papers from his apartment in Vienna, and then set fire to it. The Americans took everything from his workshop at Leonstein.

They then imprisoned Schauberger himself for several months, and released him on condition that he abandon the project. All of this is fertile ground for conspiracy theory, which has been discussed elsewhere.

There are two facts that we are certain of, but to confuse the issue even further, even they are seemingly contradictory. First, Schauberger seemed to believe in his lifetime that other people had successfully used this technology. Second, there have been many attempts to develop the suction turbine since his death, but no breakthroughs have been reported. The most successful documented attempt resulted in a 2 percent levitational effect. Hardly enough to send flying saucers into the skies.

July 15, 1936

Today we began to assemble the atom-transforming machine. Tomorrow or the day after it will run for the first time. Simple and true, that is the impression one gets when observing it.

July 24, 1936

In terms of their actual manufacture the machine's components have not been properly fabricated and now, unfortunately, I have to have the whole work carried out again completely, because I cannot achieve the required revolutions. ...

July 25, 1936

This week I checked over the machine, which intentionally or unintentionally had many faulty components. I will have nothing more to do with engineers in the future. In the final analysis they are dishonest and stupid.

July 27, 1936

*It is done! At last I have achieved planetary motion!
Wanted to smash the machine to smithereens. Inside it
everything happened contrary to my expectations ...*

*It seems as though Nature refuses to reveal her final
secret of bio-motion to me. Everything was other than
I had imagined. Something was always missing and I
really began to doubt. ...*

Excerpts from Viktor Schauberger's diary, EE, pp.125–27

9. A Material Difference

In 1933, when he had already installed several logging
flumes in central Europe, Viktor Schauberger received
an invitation from King Boris of Bulgaria to install one
in his country. The invitation was accepted, and he travelled to the country. As Schauberger was clearly a man
with wide-ranging interests and unorthodox perspectives,
King Boris asked him to investigate a phenomenon that
was beginning to trouble him. He had noticed a drop in
agricultural yields, and did not know what was behind it.

Schauberger made a tour around Bulgaria. The whole
country struck him as arid, with the vegetation struggling
for lack of water. There were deep gullies carved by the
rainwater, showing that any ran that did fall was unable
to penetrate the soil, even though it was loose and porous.
Modern steel ploughs had recently been introduced in
large parts of the country. However, in the south, near the
Turkish villages, he saw magnificent, tall stands of green
maize. He investigated further. These crops were cultivated
by the women of the households. They still used traditional wooden implements, which were too light to cut a
neat, straight modern furrow. He noticed that the clods of
earth and the wobbly lines caused by the wooden ploughs
left a pattern of light and shade on the soil. He wondered
if the choice of material, and this untidy tilling of the soil
led to such healthy crops, and if so, how.

The wisdom of the trees

The Bulgarian episode was not the first time that Viktor
Schauberger had looked for an alternative to iron. At the start
of the nineteen-thirties, when across the Rhine to the north,

the German industrial machine was going into overdrive, he decided that the healthiest, most practical way to transport water for domestic consumption was in wooden pipes, instead of iron, the material chosen by the Vienna water authorities.

He gave a list of reasons why it is unhealthy and even dangerous to bring metallic iron into contact with drinking water. Iron is a base metal. As the water passes through it, it corrodes and leaves a deposit of sediment in the pipe. This harbours harmful bacteria, which are then carried by the water. Not only that, the beneficial negative charge, which the water acquires on its upward journey through the Earth, is negated by contact with the positively-charged iron. The resulting water is flat and unhealthy. Schauberger was convinced that this would lead to in increase in disease among the drinkers of such water.

He knew that two thousand years previously, the Romans had abandoned wooden pipes as their towns grew larger. He tells how they observed the effect of the water on coins thrown into springs, and so unfortunately decided on lead, in some respects an even worse material than iron. In his view, their mistake, which he hoped to rectify, was not only the choice of metal. He felt that they should not have abandoned wood in the first place.

One of Schauberger's favourite mottoes was 'comprehend and copy' (it has more of a ring to it in the original German: *kapieren und kopieren*). As we have seen, his inspiration came from the times he spent as a young man, alone in the forests and mountains. His first formal training, and the tradition of his forebears almost as far as could be traced, was forestry. He had a great respect for the marvel of engineering technology that is a tree. He saw how trees transport water from their roots to the crown, without the use of a pump. Elsewhere, we have looked at his understandings about how this miracle of hydraulics is achieved. The material designed by Nature to carry all of this water is wood. Wood has a neutral electrical charge. It is a good electrical insulator. Kept out of the light, it does not deteriorate. Every healthy tree gives evidence that water maintains its quality as it flows through wood.

For Schauberger, Nature was alive. This means that the vessels that transport living fluids, be they a river, the wood in a tree transporting the sap, or the veins carrying the blood around our bodies, are also alive and can be more or less healthy. The process of transporting the living fluid contributes to the health of the vessel, as well as enhancing the fluid itself. Think of a river. A river interacts with its bed, building it up, repairing it and modifying its shape in a similar way that the sap flowing in a tree interacts with the living wood. Modern designs for water conduits ignored this crucial insight at their peril, he believed.

The water, therefore, has not only lost its high-grade psyche by being conducted in iron pipes, but in addition has become endowed with a pernicious and second-rate psyche.

Viktor Schauberger, WW, p.55

He had already had one success with transporting water, using wood. The wooden logging flumes that he built all over central Europe had first brought him to the attention of the wider world. He saw no reason why the same principle should not be applied to water pipes. As long as the wood was of sound quality and was bedded correctly, it should last longer than iron pipes.

Not only that, he returned to the idea he had first applied in the logging flumes after watching the water-snake swimming across the holding pool. Then, he had hurriedly had slats hammered to the sides of the channels. Now, the design was refined. Guide-vanes of silver-plated copper were attached to the inner walls of the pipe, encouraging the water to flow in a cycloid-spiral space curve. As it twists around itself, the entire twisting body of water also spirals down the pipe. Water that is encouraged to flow in such a channel becomes healthier through this motion, as its movement allows it to expel any impurities out to the periphery of the pipe. This movement energizes the water flowing down the centre of the pipe, enhancing its quality and

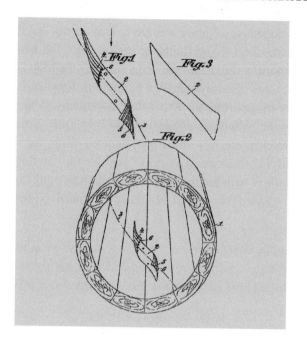

Drawing for patent 138296, guide vanes in wooden water pipe

also maintaining the health of the wood of the pipe. By the time it reaches its destination, mature, healthy drinking water flows out.

Plantation-grown timber would not be suitable for such pipes, but he calculated that there was enough timber available of the right quality, naturally grown without modern forestry techniques. He made detailed designs. He submitted patent applications. But nothing ever came of it. His idea was not taken up by the Vienna water authorities.

The incidence of cancer increases in proportion to the length of the iron water mains.

Viktor Schauberger, TFE, p.124

The Golden Plough

As we have seen, after his release by the Americans at the end of the Second World War, Viktor Schauberger was advised to stop his investigations into the suction turbine. So he turned his attention to a completely different subject, but one in which he felt the human race had taken another wrong turning: that of agriculture.

When thinking about agriculture, his starting point was that when left to her own devices, the Earth is fruitful. He pointed to the fact that a single tree produces so many seeds every season. There is a massive over-production when humans do not interfere.

One of the innovations of the early twentieth century was artificial fertilizer. Viktor Schauberger was concerned that this brought short-term benefits, but ultimately clogged up the soil. It brought a short-term spurt of growth, but at long-term cost. He referred to it as a stimulant obtained from blast-furnace slag. He acknowledged that its components are of benefit to the plants, but believed that its electrical properties are not. It has been de-energized by fire, and so will rob the soil of energy, just as a glass of flat water drains the drinker and an iron plough drains the soil. For these reasons, he believed that artificial fertilizer and iron agricultural implements both represented wrong turnings, preventing the Earth from being as fruitful as it could be.

If artificial fertilizer is spread, then the slag-residues, utterly devoid of potential due to the annihilating influences of fire, rob the groundwater of its levitative and stimulating substances. The biological consequence of this violent system of replenishment is a phoney productivity, which delivers a great deal of material but leaves little if any nutritive value in the soil.

Viktor Schauberger, TFE, p.174

Der Biopflug

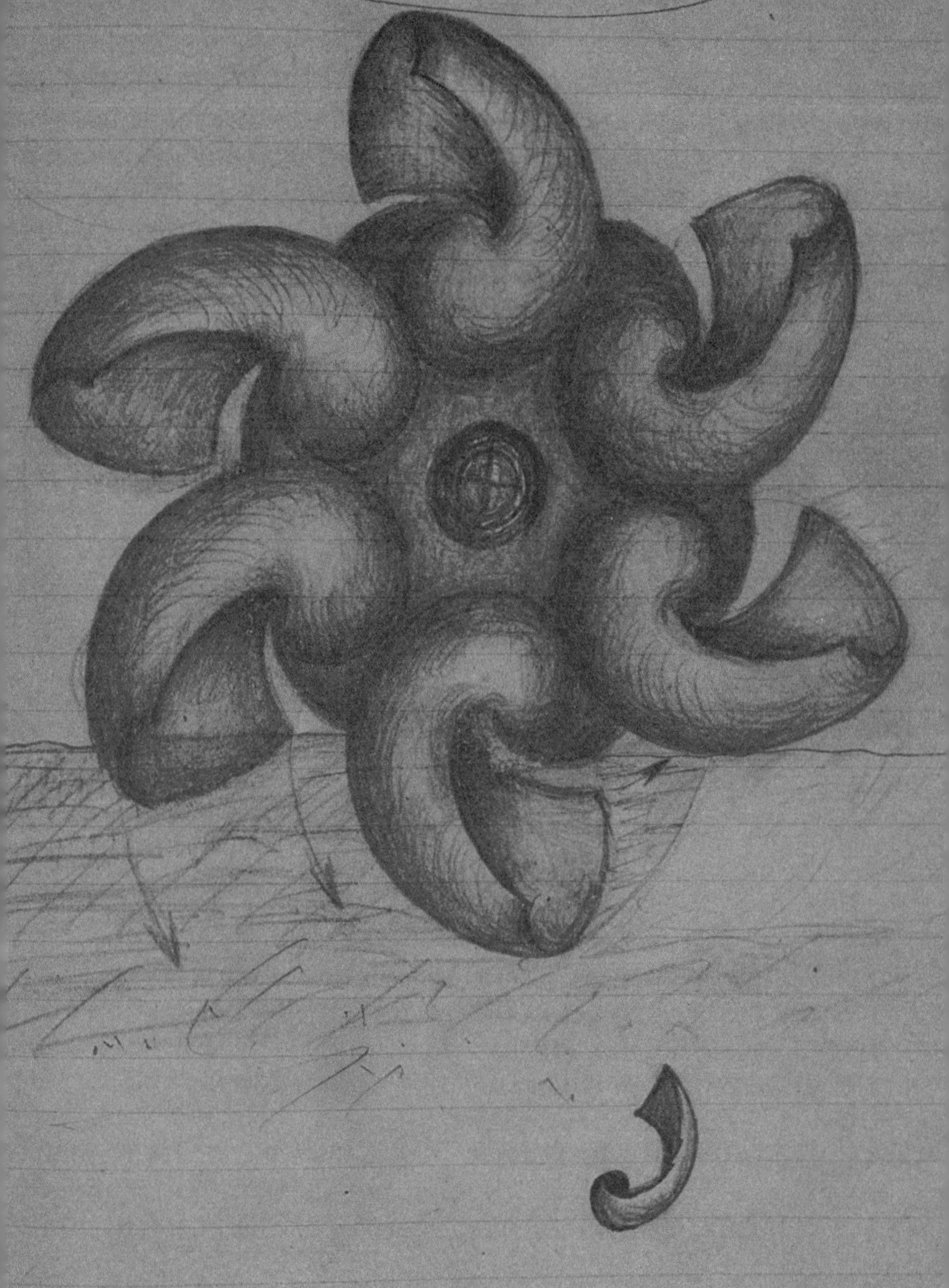

His visit to Bulgaria in the 1930s had given him the idea that all of the reasons he had advanced against the use of metallic iron for transporting water had equal validity when applied to agricultural implements. He thought that bringing iron into contact with the groundwater would be damaging to the health of the soil and the plants. Contact with iron drains the water of any charge it carries, and as iron is a base metal, it also corrodes. As already noted, in Viktor Schauberger's view, this allows harmful bacteria to proliferate. Finally, using iron ploughs dries out the soil. The positively-charged iron cancels out the negative charge in the geosphere, and also decomposes the groundwater. Ultimately, in his view, this leads to a drop in the water table. He described the effect of using iron ploughs as spreading a puerperal fever, the fever of childbirth over the land.

Iron and steel, which have been polarized by fire, are very dangerous to forest and field alike, because these discharged substances attract the valuable soil-energies like a magnet.

Viktor Schauberger, TFE, p.124

For implements, he looked for an alternative to iron, and settled on copper. He gave two reasons for his choice of copper. First, minerals containing copper, such as malachite, are water-retentive. Second, he saw that where the soil had copper ores present, there was thriving vegetation. Further reasons, which he did not explicitly state, are that copper is hardened by cold rather than heat as is the case with iron, it is non-magnetic, and so does not disturb soil magnetism. Finally, copper has high thermal and electrical conductivity.

◄ *The spiral plough. Drawing by Viktor Schauberger.*

This means that any soil energies that come into contact with copper are not drained as they are when they meet metallic iron, but are assisted in their flow and are available to nourish the plants.

In 1947 he was ready to conduct field trials. He had the support of a qualified agricultural scientist, Franz Rosenberger, who was the independent witness on four of the trials. Three of the trials were carried out in association with the Chief Agronomist of the Salzburg Primary Industry Department. Several sites around Salzburg were selected. The plan was to cultivate alternate strips in the same fields with a conventional steel plough and a plough with copper-plated shares. In all other respects the strips would be treated identically. A variety of crops were chosen. Grain crops included barley, oats and rye; root crops included carrots and potatoes, and green fodder crops selected were clover, grass and silage maize.

Transferring an idea to reality is often tricky, and inevitably the trials were beset with practical problems. For some of them, a steel plough was not used as a control. In others, the crop was harvested and processed without being weighed and measured. In these instances, the monitors relied on previous observation of the crops in the fields and made estimates of the yield. However, despite these inconveniences the outcome was clear and consistent. For all of the plants cultivated, the strips cultivated with the copper-plated plough had larger, healthier plants, fewer pests and significantly higher yields than the control strips. The remarkable copper-plated plough came to be known as the 'Golden Plough.'

But then things started to go wrong. Viktor Schauberger designed a new plough and wanted to go into commercial production. However, there were many people who were satisfied with the status quo, and who were in a position to permit or prevent the project from advancing. Developing such a new venture requires delicate diplomatic skills, skills which Schauberger never showed any sign of possessing. He himself admitted that he did not even get the farmers on his side. They were worried that overproduction resulting from the use of the new plough would depress prices. The story, reported later by Viktor Schauberger's son, is that the final straw came when an official informed him that the fertilizer companies had made it financially worth his while to encourage the use of their products. This plough would reduce the need for fertilizer. Would Viktor Schauberger be willing to enter into a similar arrangement, in which the official would promote the use of the plough in exchange for an appropriate recompense? The answer was a definite 'No.' Schauberger immediately ended the conversation, declaring that he did not make deals with criminals. Perhaps not surprisingly, it then became very difficult for him to obtain any copper, and he was forced to abandon the project.

Farmers feared a considerable reduction in the price of their produce, even though in the first year they achieved about a sixty percent increase in yield. The only advantage the farmers acknowledged was the elimination of high pest-control costs, since, as is the case in any naturally healthy forest, no parasite can continue to survive (there).

Viktor Schauberger, TFE, p.72

Healing the land

He saw other possibilities for copper. He heard about a tradition in southern Russia, in which the Tartars hung copper strips and pipes in the channels carrying the water destined for their fields. This enlivened the water. He developed the idea, and advised storing water for the fields in an egg-shaped container, made of clay, earthenware, glass or wood.

If a wooden barrel, the iron hoops should be removed and replaced with copper or wooden ones. Then copper and zinc, hammered on to pieces of wood, should be placed in the container. Ideally it should be two metres deep, and buried in the ground with the pointy end uppermost. Leave a small hole at the top and cover it with linen or canvas, so that only diffuse oxygen enters the container. The water contained in such a vessel would emit a healthy radiation through the surrounding land.

However, iron does have its uses. Viktor Schauberger tells how farmers used to protect the blooms in their orchards from late frosts, by spraying water through iron or steel nozzles. This raises the temperature in the crown zone, and as the sprayed air has a different charge, it does not mix with the surrounding, much colder air. Copper has the opposite effect to iron. The converse of this process, spraying through copper nozzles, cools the air and so protects young shoots from scorching.

Any human interventions should assist the natural processes of growth, decay and renewal, in which the Earth reincorporates the remains of the preceding generations in order to give life to the next. Rather than covering the land with this waste-product of the chemical industry, he advocated sprinkling it with energized water and compost that has completed its cycle of cold fermentation. Together with the use of copper implements, this system would mean that agriculture could be so productive that the human race would then never have to go hungry again.

These reactive forces are available in almost unlimited quantity, due to higher-grade fermentation processes produced by the naturally-fermented fatty residues of deceased life-forms in the anomaly zone. This also explains how, from the minutest seed, a gigantic tree can arise, which itself creates a thousand million seeds. A properly planted potato can produce up to 20kg (44lbs) of high-quality potatoes within half a year if one merely remembers to incorporate the type of negatively-charged catalyst required for every type of transformation.

Viktor Schauberger, NAT, p.97

10. The Inheritance, the Inspiration and the Vision

Den Sinnen hast du dann zu trauen,
Kein Falsches lassen sie dich schauen,
Wenn dein Verstand dich wach erhalt,

Mit frischen Blick bemerke freudig.
Und wandle, sicher wie geschmeidig.
Durch Auen reichbegabter Welt.

(Next, you must trust your senses:
They will show you nothing false
If your intelligence keeps you awake.

Keep your eyes open and fresh and joyful,
And move with sure steps, yet flexibly,
Through the fields of a world so richly endowed.)

Johann Wolfgang von Goethe, quoted in Naydler,
Goethe on Science

Viktor Schauberger acknowledged his debt to the great thinkers who had preceded him. He had a particular respect for Goethe, whom he referred to as the Prince of Poetry. He frequently quoted the last line of Goethe's epic play *Faust*:

The Eternal Feminine draws us onwards
(Das ewig Weibliche zieht uns hinan)

For Viktor Schauberger, this phrase summed up one of the fundamental facts of our lives, the unceasing movement of original motion.

Johann Wolfgang von Goethe was born in Frankfurt in 1749 and died in 1832. For English speakers, it is difficult to appreciate the huge legacy of Goethe in the German-speaking world. His writings are not easily translated into English, and he bestrides so many categories. After a wild youth (known as the *Sturm und Drang,* 'storm and urge,' years), he became the principal administrator of the duchy of Weimar. This sounds grand, but Weimar was small and decidedly off the beaten track at the time. However, Goethe put it on the map. He became known throughout Europe as a man of letters: a scientist, philosopher, poet, playwright and novelist. Napoleon made a point of visiting him. He advocated a holistic system of scientific understanding, against the reductionist current of the Enlightenment thinking of the time.

His writings are collated into 143 volumes. This book is about Viktor Schauberger, not Goethe, so here we will select just two of Schauberger's ideas that have resonances from Goethe.

The whole of nature

As we have seen, Viktor Schauberger understood water as the 'blood of the Earth' (a phrase first used by Goethe), and the Earth as a living entity. All that exists on the Earth is subject to change, as part of this living, breathing whole. This sets the tone of his enquiry. Rather than an inert set of elements to be analysed in the laboratory, the Earth is alive, and to be appreciated with all of our senses.

Such an approach fits closely with Goethe's view. For Goethe, the danger of microscopes and telescopes is that they allow us to perceive an even smaller segment of reality than that permitted by our already limited senses. After all, the human eye perceives only a small section of the vast electromagnetic spectrum. Our ears, also, are tuned to a pick up small range of all that exists. But considered in their entirety, our senses can make an instrument which is more perceptive than any machine. Our task is then to be able to trust the process, and grasp what our senses show us, as Viktor Schauberger did when he let his consciousness flow with the water of the mountain stream, in the story at the beginning of this book.

The reality behind appearances

One idea of Goethe's in particular resonates throughout Viktor Schauberger's understandings. This is the concept of the *Urphenomenon,* the original or archetype. In line with Goethe's thinking, Schauberger looked for the archetype, the essential quality of the phenomena he observed. He describes planetary motion as original or archetypal motion. Both the movement of the planets in the heavens and flow of the water in a stream reflect this archetypal movement. The egg-shape is another archetype. Every new life springs forth from an egg, and each one is a different echo of the underlying archetypal egg. The closer one comes to seeing behind the examples of form and to understanding the archetype behind them all, the nearer one is to the truth. In Goethe's own words:

> No organic being wholly corresponds to the underlying idea. The higher idea lurks behind each. This is my God; that is the God we all seek and hope to set our countenance upon; but we can only divine him, not see him. *(Goethe, quoted in Naydler, 2000, p.109)*

The cause of movement

Going several centuries further back, Viktor Schauberger acknowledges the contributions made to learning by Leonardo da Vinci and Paracelsus. Both of these men were self-taught original thinkers and observers of Nature, like Schauberger himself. He frequently refers to a phrase of Da Vinci's: *Il Primo Motore,* the First Cause or Prime Mover. Da Vinci was interested in the urge towards balance in Nature: the way a force applied to an object will translate into movement and equal itself out. If the movement is interrupted, the object will bounce and continue its movement until the original impetus is exhausted. Schauberger was also fascinated by the mystery of movement, particularly the cycloid-spiral space-curve.

Analysis or synthesis?

The idea of the archetype or *Ur-phenomenon* as described by Goethe can be traced back to Plato. Goethe was very interested in classical Greek thinking, and Viktor Schauberger also made reference to the Greeks in his writings. Schauberger placed great importance on intuitive insights, as did Goethe, the Greeks and many thinkers in the years between. In his view such a form of perception offers a profound, holistic appreciation of the processes of life, in contrast to rational thought alone, which can only give an incomplete picture of reality. Here is his explanation of the difference between the scientific method as applied in the twentieth century and the tradition that he saw himself to be part of:

> *The basic teaching of the Ionic natural philosopher Thales (625–545 BC), 'Water is the source of all Life,' embodies a profound understanding and is of great importance. It should in no way be construed as idle speculation. As a Greek, he had intuition, which according to Goethe is 'a revelation emanating from the inner self.' Intuition is spiritual seeing, not an insight gained through experience or rational thought. According to Spinoza, it is the highest form of perception because the pure principles of Nature alone remain active and*

the categorizing propensity (compart-mentality) of the human mind does not come into action. ...

Viktor Schauberger, WW, p.15

However, it has to be said that Viktor Schauberger used both systems of thinking in his own work. From his times alone in the mountains he acquired insights, which he then was able to understand further through rational analysis. This in turn led to the inventions. The important thing for him was that the intuitive appreciation came first.

The words 'analysis' and 'synthesis' can be applied to both the realms of ideas and of physical reality. The original Greek sense of analysis is to unloose, to separate into simpler elements. Its opposite is synthesis, meaning composition: the process from simpler principles to complex consequences. For Viktor Schauberger, analysis is what happens with decomposition and technical motion. Synthesis describes the miracle that occurs in the growth of a tree. As both processes together form the pulse of Nature, so both are needed for our thinking and understanding to move on. It was Viktor Schauberger's belief that when these two processes are in the correct equilibrium then a third process, the unceasing onward motion of life itself can have its expression.

The flow of existence

He shared his reverence for water with Heraclitus, one of the earliest known Greek philosophers, most of whose writings have been lost. Heraclitus was known as 'the obscure' by his successors, as some of his sayings were so cryptic, the following being a good example: 'For souls it is death to become water, for water death to become earth; but from earth water comes into being, from water soul.'

Compare this with one of Viktor Schauberger's more enigmatic utterances:

Air-eggs produce water
Water-eggs produce earth
Earth-eggs produce energy-eggs (dynagens)

Both men were fascinated by the flow of life, the unceasing motion that we see around us. The direction of the process described is different, but there is a similarity of approach between the writings of these two men, separated by two millennia.

It was Heraclitus, who long ago stated that one cannot bathe in the same water twice, because it is in continual motion even when apparently still, and is thus in a constant state of metamorphosis.

Viktor Schauberger, EE, p.99

However, Schauberger believed that he had rediscovered ideas that could be traced back even further, to the time of Atlantis. The technology behind his inventions was known, understood and applied by the Ancients, he believed. In fact, he asserts that misuse of it was behind the catastrophe of Atlantis. They so over-stimulated these formative energies that whole sections of the Earth were wrenched skywards.

Viktor Schauberger's inspiration

Viktor Schauberger saw his work as nurturing the flame of learning. He carried the baton from the great thinkers of the past into the present. This learning shows a way for humans to live in harmony with planet Earth, our present home.

Untitled drawing by Viktor Schauberger ➤

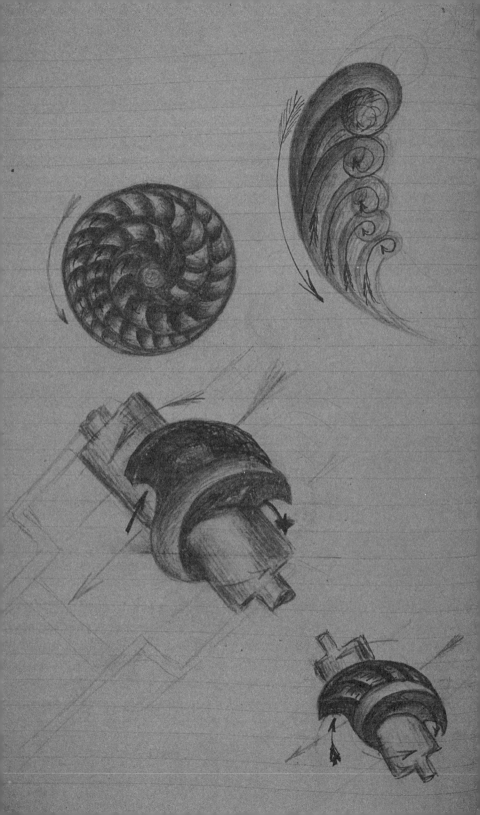

He was a forester and a hunter, used to his own company. As a young man he spent hours alone in the wild places, observing the processes quietly unfolding around him. If you have ever been in the forests, away from where humans are, you will know that they are big. Trees are big, as are mountains. Mountain streams are powerful. In such an environment, a person can only reflect that of Nature and humans, Nature is by far the more powerful, more caring, more marvellous. Nature achieves miraculous things in peace and silence, which are there for us all to see when we take the time. After spending time in such places, most modern human creations, such as roads, factories and towns, will look and feel like dead bits of skin, a cancer on the landscape.

This is where Viktor Schauberger's inspiration came from. He spent hours watching the way the water curls in a stream, and when he returned home, he tried to draw what he had seen. He then saw the same patterns elsewhere, in the way a tree grows and a running wild animal passes water. Eventually, these drawings developed into the models for his inventions.

He talked to the mountain men, who themselves had spent their lives in the forests and mountains and had learnt from what they saw. He learned that if an older man drinks the water of a high mountain spring, he will be sexually vigorous. He saw that the trout return to the same high streams in the spawning season, leaping up waterfalls in their desire to be there. He saw that the mountain goats return to such places when they are unwell, to eat the healing herbs that grow nearby. He then tried to make sense of these observations, to discover what was so special about the water in these places.

If he had stayed in the mountains, working as a forester and learning from what he saw, he would have led a fulfilling life and no one would know anything about him beyond his immediate circle. He would probably have been known as a wise and interesting old man with some strange views.

But an idea grew in him, about where humanity had taken a wrong turning and how human life could be, so that everyone could have the chance to live in the protection of Nature, the way that the life of the forest does. We don't have to fight Nature — we are all part of life. He saw a part of how this could be done. He saw the processes that Nature uses, and realized that we can use them too. Nature is a net creator, not destroyer. Humans can be the same.

It started with the logging flumes, which so went against the grain of conventional thinking. Despite not taking the shortest route and involving other idiosyncratic considerations such as the temperature of the water, they worked, very efficiently. The design was subtle and precise. Others tried to imitate their design, but did not succeed. From this success, Schauberger realized that other devices could be built, which would be a boon to all of humanity. He devised river-regulation methods which allowed the river to control itself. Later, he developed devices to produce drinking water of the quality of springwater, and levitational machines.

Living with the knowing, this vision of how life could be, it broke his heart to see what the river authorities did to the Danube and the Rhine. Their management strategies were based on the concept that water is inert. He saw the rivers as part of a living entirety, and tried his best to persuade the authorities to see what he saw. Plantation forestry practices broke his heart, too. He saw clearly the damage that they perpetrated across the whole ecosystem.

The vision

Planet Earth is finite. Matter cannot be created or destroyed: it can only change its form. As everything we see is in process, matter is continually changing its form. Viktor Schauberger places great significance on the direction of change: downwards, through destruction and decomposition into its simpler components, or upwards, through refinement and growth.

The predominant process has an effect on all living things. If the former process is in the ascendant, then the overriding impulse is one of decay. It means that plants cannot grow healthily, so there is increased hunger and distress all the way up the chain of life. This is what he observed in the world around him, which in his view was a direct consequence of the human race's dependence on destructive technology. The human lot is seen as hard labour, motivated by fear.

His vision was that it does not have to be like that. Nature can provide all that we need, for an improving, enhancing quality of life. Nature uses creative more than destructive energies, and has had a lot of practice at it. The very essence of Mother Earth lives to nurture, protect and uplift. This can be felt if one stands silent in a forest glade. A forest can be seen as a gigantic machine, processing Sun energy and Earth energy, marrying them together for the enhancement and progression of all in its ambit. We, too, can be protected and sustained, when we have respect for and understanding of Nature's ways, and order our lives in the light of this understanding.

For Schauberger, the way to realize this dream is by replacing existing technology with the one that he had rediscovered from observing the way that Nature works. Others in the modern era had discovered it before him, but had been prevented from applying it. He names John Worrell Keely and John Andrew in the USA at the turn of the twentieth century. This technology is based predominantly on creation, not destruction. Not only is it more efficient, the use of it is beneficial, enhancing, ennobling to all of life, including the Earth itself.

In the future Mother Earth will again be able quietly to build up her energizing substances in all peace, which today are so foolishly combusted.

Viktor Schauberger, WW, p.164

At the time of Atlantis the knowledge was only known to a few, the initiates, and so was lost. He did not want that to happen again.

He saw his own role as twofold — to develop the technology, and to educate others in the underlying principles so that future generations would be able to work with it too. It would not be lost to humanity as it had been in the past.

This second part of his role required him to present a world view which was as different from what is taught in our schools and colleges as planetary is from technical motion. He did it partly by means of stories from his own experience, and partly by developing a system to explain what he saw at play.

But it is also an inseparable part of Viktor Schauberger's world view that this technology is only accessible to those who have a reverence for life and a concern for the common good. Certainly, in his lifetime and since, very few people have been able to exploit his ideas for commercial profit or personal gain.

The implosion machines ... can only be entrusted to those who place the common good before their own wellbeing. They should have absolutely no interest in clinging to any kind of craving for power.

Viktor Schauberger, TFE, p.34

He foresaw a world in which there is so much plenty that there is no need for war. No one needs to go hungry. Charity and tolerance will be the most rational motives for human behaviour. Humanity will resume its upward evolutionary path.

Humanity, by nature never a beast of burden, will be delivered from all labour with my machine.

Viktor Schauberger, NAT, p.31

Viktor Schauberger was a simple man. He believed that he had found the solution to humanity's problems. He believed that the truth would out, that sooner or later the decision-makers would see what was so obvious to him. It only remained for them to apply the technology he had discovered, for the benefit of all.

Through the rebirth of spirit, humanity will become accustomed to revere and care for all life arising anew out of the Earth.

                              Viktor Schauberger, NAT, p.32

Towards the end of his life he began to suspect that the truths which burned in him were in danger of dying with him. The salvation of the human race was being rejected by those who could implement it. This was a great disappointment to him. My own suspicion is that this is part of the reason why he agreed to go to America in the last year of his life. It was a final chance to leave something for future generations.

Was it a higher direction of events or a remarkable accident that led to the revelation of evolution's most profound secret, a secret that has lain buried for thousands of years, by of all things the most silent creature on this Earth? It was a trout floating motionlessly amidst the torrential waters of an alpine stream that divulged it to a young forester with an inherited gift of an intimate connection with Nature.

                              Viktor Schauberger, TFE, p.29

11. Passing the Baton

Viktor Schauberger's son, Walter, told an extraordinary story about an incident that had happened to his father in 1938.

As a condition of his war pension, from being wounded in the First World War, Viktor Schauberger had to attend a brief medical examination once every three years. When his appointment fell due in 1938, the Germans had already occupied Vienna. Before going to the clinic, he met a friend, Mrs Mada Primavesi, for coffee. He then excused himself, saying the appointment would only take about twenty minutes. She agreed to wait for him.

After an hour and a half, and four cups of coffee, Schauberger had not returned and Mrs Primavesi began to be concerned. She rang his home, but he had not gone there. Knowing that he was not a man to break his word, she then went to the clinic to find out what had happened. Nobody could tell her where he was. Mrs Primavesi then demanded of the director of the clinic, whom she knew socially, that they make a room-by-room search. Schauberger was eventually found in the lunatic section, trussed up in a straitjacket and lying quietly on a bed inside a steel cage, surrounded by noisier inmates in other cages. Already at that time, the story goes, it was the procedure to dispose of people deemed undesirable to the Third Reich by means of a lethal injection.

Schauberger was quickly released. The director of the clinic apologized profusely and wrote a letter, confirming his sanity.

Presumably this story was told to Walter by his father. Walter evidently believed it, and his widow, Frau Ingeborg Schauberger, also confirmed that she believed

it to be true. Viktor himself did not directly refer to
the incident in his writings. He had been so relentlessly
critical of the status quo for so many years, that even he
acknowledged that he had acquired enemies along the
way. But this does seem an extreme way to silence a critic.

Recognition at last?

Viktor Schauberger had many reasons to be disillusioned with
the powers that be. The story above is an extreme example. He
suspected that at times his ideas had been taken by others. There
is a suggestion that during the war, Heinkel was able to get a
sneak preview of one of his patent applications and make use of
it himself. The blocking of his project with the golden plough
was a familiar experience, the latest frustration in a long series.

After abandoning the plough project, Schauberger took a new
look at one of his earlier interests. With his new appreciation
of the importance of materials, he refined his designs for water
pipes. He looked at spiralling shapes in nature. If you take an animal horn such as that of the kudu antelope, and slice it through,
the cross-section has the profile of an egg with a bite taken out
at the side of the blunt end. He experimented with water flow
through copper pipes, twisted into a similar configuration.

In 1952 Viktor Schauberger had the opportunity to demonstrate this line of research at the University of Stuttgart.
Professor Franz Popel of the Institute of Hygiene reluctantly
agreed to carry out some investigations on water flow in pipes
of various shapes and materials. In fact, he initially asked to
withdraw from the trials, saying that he could not see that they
would achieve any useful results. He was persuaded to remain
by a representative of the German Water Resources Ministry,
on the grounds that it might put a stop to Schauberger's attacks
on their methods of river management. Even so, he agreed to
investigate only a portion of the tests requested by Schauberger,
and this at Schauberger's personal expense.

The first test was seemingly innocuous. Water was poured out of a holding vessel into a narrow glass pipe, so that it formed a vortex, just as water does when it flows out of a bath into a narrow plughole. Before pouring the water, a thin silk thread with copper filaments, weighted at the bottom, was suspended in the pipe. The investigators then watched the movement of the thread, as it slowly rotated in a space-curve in the centre of the vortex, as predicted by Schauberger. Conventional wisdom said that the thread would be pushed to the side of the pipe by centrifugal motion. The fact that it didn't was the first surprise for Professor Popel.

Next, three silk threads were suspended in the pipe. They were attached to each corner of a triangular block, fixed by spacers in the middle and towards the lower end, and weighted at the bottom. Although the threads had less freedom of movement than the single thread, they too swayed in the spiral flow of water down the pipe. Not only that, they entwined around each other as the water flowed. The investigators wondered if the spacers caused the twining, so these were removed and water was poured in again. Still the threads twined when the water flowed. The investigators conceded that this behaviour of the threads was new to science. They noticed a darkening of the water around the filaments, as if less light was coming from the water around them. They concluded that mechanical forces alone — centrifugal and centripetal motion — could not account for these phenomena. They could only be explained if electrical processes were also at play.

In the next batch of tests, water was poured into pipes of different shapes and materials, and the rate of flow was measured. The test was narrowed down to three pipes: a straight glass pipe, a straight copper pipe, and a copper pipe shaped into decreasing spirals, like the kudu horn. Water flowing through the glass pipe showed the greatest resistance, and greatest friction. The straight copper pipe showed less, and the spiral copper pipe defied expectations. At one point, the measuring devices recorded zero or even negative friction in the water flowing through this pipe. This violates one of the sacred canons of science, the second law of thermodynamics, that a closed system will run down without a further input of energy. In Franz Popel's own words:

> The interpretation and evaluation of the observa-
> tions selected above hence also permit the hypo-
> thetical conclusion, that the synchronization of
> the kinetic energy of the flowing water generates
> more energy due to the spiralling and twisting of
> the pipes than is required to overcome the fric-
> tional losses obtaining. A constantly increasing
> acceleration in the flow of the water would have
> to occur. (Prof. Franz Popel, 15 March 1952,
> quoted in EE, p.243)

This vindicates so much of what Viktor Schauberger had been saying, for so many years. It explains the success of his logging flumes, thirty years previously. It says that the river management policies of the Rhine and Danube were indeed wrong-headed. It means that cutting off the meanders in a river will not increase its rate of flow, as he had repeatedly pointed out. It says that reinforcing the banks of a river is not the best way to manage its flow. It shows that when original motion is encouraged in a pipe, it will not clog up, as the heavier materials are carried down the centre of the vortex. At last, here was independent confirmation of a central part of Viktor Schauberger's system, the significance, relevance and scope for application of the principle of original motion.

However, the human race shows a remarkable ability to ignore facts that do not fit in with the received wisdom, and the academic community is no exception to this. It was deemed that the trials had yielded interesting preliminary results, which warranted further investigation. In the absence of funding, the further investigation never happened.

Alone again

Despite a lack of funds, Viktor Schauberger carried on by himself, looking for applications of this technology. He worked with the principles he had discovered, that had been a constant theme throughout his adult life. Whereas all modern machines generate power through pressure, heat and expansion, Schauberger relied on the opposite process: suction instead of pressure, cooling instead of heating, and winding inwards instead of outwards.

His machines were intended to work with air or water. They required a small initial input of power to start off a process of in-winding flow which cools the water or air, thereby causing a falling temperature gradient towards the anomaly point, which in turn creates a biological vacuum. This then draws in more air or water behind it, at an ever-increasing rate. The resulting turbine could be used to generate power, or to produce high quality, health-giving drinking water.

One such application was the domestic power station. It is based on the suction turbine described earlier, and has some additional components. The centre of it consists of a swirl of copper pipes. From the horizontal plane, they twist inwards towards a central point, from which they continue to spiral around each other on the vertical plane, almost like the sap vessels in a tree trunk. These take up the water as it exits from the suction turbine. Above them is an inlet pipe. The entrance to the pipe alternately opens and closes as the pipes rotate underneath it, ever faster and faster. The temporary vacuums caused by the oscillating movement in this machine would allow almost a nine-fold increase in power to be generated, he believed.

Viktor Schauberger did not have enough funds to fully develop the domestic power station. He himself said that on twelve occasions the authorities had taken his ideas from him by for their own use, and so he was not inclined to share them with people who could help him. This hampered his efforts even further, leaving him lonely, disappointed and frustrated.

To the end of his days he burned with the importance of his discoveries. The use of technology based on decomposition was detrimental to all of humanity, leading us on a downward path with an increasing incidence of disease, particularly cancer. He even began to wonder if the authorities deliberately taught this dangerous technology in the schools and universities. This made him even more wary of publicizing his findings too widely. He wanted his ideas to survive, to be available for future generations to use. As planet Earth moves ever onwards in her in-winding spiralling path, so the future generations of humanity are evolutionarily older, and so, he believed, may be able to appreciate the vital importance of his discoveries.

The son and heir

Viktor Schauberger's son Walter, who had accompanied him to the University of Stuttgart in 1952, had an academic background. He had trained as a physicist, and by the 1950s had begun to appreciate the importance of his father's work.

Viktor was not an easy man to live with. Because of his mistrust of academia, he also mistrusted his son's ability to understand his work. Walter gave up his academic career to help his father, and still Viktor would not open up to him. However, they did attempt some joint ventures. In 1949 they set up in Austria what may have been the first modern Green political party: the Green Front. It voiced the concerns of the green parties that were to follow — nuclear power, deforestation, river management, and warned of the dangers if we did not curb our excesses — climate change and pollution.

On one occasion, Walter went to the Department of Agriculture at the University of Vienna to present his father's ideas. On his return, he and his wife Ingeborg had tea with

◀ *Untitled drawing by Viktor Schauberger*

Viktor. According to Frau Ingeborg, Walter told them both about the visit, and said how pleased he was to have the chance to explain Viktor's ideas to the academic world, and the positive response he had received. Viktor's reaction was angry: 'What have you done? You spoil the whole thing! Those ignorant people will never understand my work!'

Frau Ingeborg came to her husband's defence, explaining that she believed her husband was right to do this. Viktor was surprised that she stood by her husband, and never argued with him in front of her again.

This incident is perhaps made more poignant by a disappointment in Viktor Schauberger's life. He did not have the same level of support and understanding with his own wife. In time, he came around to the viewpoint that it was a good thing that Walter spoke to the academics. This was something that he himself had been quite patently unable to do.

Viktor Schauberger repeatedly said that what he was proposing was not difficult. We only have to do what Nature is already doing, all around us all the time. It's only a small step, and we just have to find the key. Another thing he used to say was, 'I have a secret, and nobody is worthy to receive it.' Not even his own son was deemed worthy. Whatever his secret was, he took it with him to the grave.

Walter accompanied his father to the USA in 1958. As we have seen, this trip was very costly for Viktor, who was by then an elderly man. On their return from Texas, Viktor went home to Linz and Walter back to his home in Bad Ischl, several hours away. Walter shut himself away, announcing that he did not want to be disturbed. A few days later came the news that Viktor had died.

What next?

One can only try to imagine the effect his father's sudden death had on Walter. His wife Ingeborg has said that it was a great shock to him. How should he continue? On one hand, he had come to realize the importance of his father's work. On the other, his father had never considered him the right person to advance it. Indeed, Viktor had made it very clear that he had never found a suitable candidate. Would this valuable body of work come to a halt? Frau Ingeborg herself appreciated the significance of Viktor's legacy, and felt that Walter was the man to take up the baton. She advised Walter to take it on: it was his task now. She would support him.

Walter saw his role as consisting of several elements. One was to rehabilitate his father's reputation. Many people dismissed Viktor as a crackpot. As we have seen, Walter had the academic stature to present his father's ideas in an accessible way. He had already begun this work, and won his father's reluctant approval for it, in Viktor's lifetime. He travelled overseas in this work, too. Richard St Barbe Baker, founder of the International Men of the Trees, arranged for him to give a lecture at Birmingham University in the UK in 1951. Walter had friends who were editors of journals, and so was able to have some of his articles published.

However, he soon ran into problems with this approach. Many people were fascinated and supportive in private, but refused to say so in public. Viktor's ideas were so unconventional and outside the mainstream that they feared that supporting them would endanger their own careers.

Walter abandoned his excursion into politics and the Green Front. He came to the view that the system he was propounding transcended politics. Every political party should have its green people, he said.

The Pythagoras-Kepler-System

Walter was by inclination a mathematician. He looked for a mathematical way to describe the forms his father used in his inventions. He showed the mathematical relationship between the egg-shape and the hyperbolic curve. In effect, he had to develop a new branch of mathematics in order to do this.

He set up an organization, the Pythagoras-Kepler-System or PKS, to promote his own and his father's work. He presented these findings in seminars, which he organized through the PKS. People from various disciplines came to the seminars: engineers, ecologists, inventors and entrepreneurs. He was convinced that the elimination of all technology is not the way forward for the human race, and searched for ways in which Nature and technology can work together. The underlying theme of the seminars was to discover ways to champion the woodland and the water, to find a human-scale technology that is not destructive to the Earth.

This second strand to Walter's work was not without its frustrations. He looked for a way forward, and many people he worked with harked back to the past. More than once he was told, 'What you say is interesting, but your father said ...' However, he was determined not to make his father into a guru, and so he stayed focussed on ways to progress the ideas and the priorities that both he and his father had agreed about.

The seminars had their successes. Walter was a communicator, a compelling speaker. People went away inspired. Unlike his father, he was able to encourage people to develop their own ideas arising from Viktor's insights. Walter saw his own role as staying at the centre, elucidating the principles of the system. It was for others to find the applications. And through Walter's work, his father's ideas found their way into developments in milk processing, water treatment, river management and more.

He worked with a Swedish friend, Olof Alexandersson, who wrote a small and inspiring book telling the story of Viktor Schauberger. This was later translated into English, and so Viktor Schauberger's system of thinking spread beyond the German-speaking world.

By the end of Walter's life, his father's name was known all over the world. Individuals were experimenting with the ideas he proposed, with varying degrees of success. Perhaps Walter's greatest achievement is that he ensured that his own and his father's voices were added to the stream of dissent against prevailing agricultural trends. They were among those who kept alive the idea of the Earth as a living entity, to be treated with respect, during the barren agro-industry years from the nineteen-fifties to the eighties.

Walter Schauberger and a PKS seminar group

12. Into the Twenty-first Century

A smooth transition

Frau Schauberger's secretary, Wolfgang Prock, took over the reins of PKS after Walter's death in 1997. Continuing the work of spreading the ideas and taking advantage of new technology, he compiled a CD containing Viktor's ideas about water. He also re-instituted the PKS seminars, which had lapsed towards the end of Walter's life. In 1999, Walter and Ingeborg's son, Jörg, gave up his career in the media to come back to the PKS. As he had studied Mathematics and Physics at university, he is well placed to continue the work of bringing his father's and grandfather's ideas to the attention of a wider audience.

The ripples spread

Walter's work to spread the word about his father's work continues to have an effect, even more so now in the age of the internet. There are individuals working to apply Viktor Schauberger's ideas all over the world, from Sweden to Australia, South Korea to the USA. There have been particular successes with water treatment methods.

There was also a parallel development. A fellow Austrian, a generation older than Viktor Schauberger, gave a series of lectures in 1924, proposing a new approach to agriculture. This series of lectures by Rudolf Steiner was the cornerstone of the biodynamic agriculture movement and only one example of a new approach to holistic science. Inspired by Steiner's insights, researchers like Theodor Schwenk, George Adams and John Wilkes started to look at the way water flows, and independently came to similar conclusions to Viktor Schauberger. They developed Flowforms, watercourses that encouraged the flow-ing water to wind in and around itself, and this water was found to have beneficial properties for plants and water life.

In some ways, the times have caught up with Viktor Schauberger. His ideas on river management have now started to come into the mainstream. In the case of the Rhine, there were two major floods and a serious poisoning incident before they did so. In 1986 a fire at a chemical plant on the bank of the river Rhine led to serious pollution of the river. Dead fish were washed up on the banks a hundred miles downstream, in the Netherlands. This was a wake-up call, which was reinforced by the extensive floods of 1993 and 1995. In 1998 Ministers of the European Union agreed on an action plan for flood defence of the Rhine. It incorporates the ideas that embank-ments cannot guarantee protection from flooding, that the river must be allowed to overflow its banks, particularly in the upper reaches. Forestry is also seen as a crucial ingredient of river management. It would seem that Viktor Schauberger's motto, 'Comprehend and Copy,' is at last being applied.

Enlightenment has spread, although haltingly, through improved forestry practices, too. In the UK, the great storm of October 1987 provided a stimulus. It was found that plantation-grown conifers fared less well than the original broad-leaved woodland. Not only that, it was noticed that woodland areas that were left alone regenerated more quickly than replanted areas. By the turn of the twenty-first century, the proportion of conifers to broadleaved woodland in the UK was back to the level it had been fifty years previously. These are developments that would have gladdened Viktor Schauberger's heart, although he would probably have found plenty more to criticize. There is also a movement away from the practice of clear-felling, although not for the reasons propounded by Viktor Schauberger. It is now recognized that the practice leads to disruption in the ecosystem, and a new term, 'continuous cover' forestry, has entered the vocabulary of woodland management.

Some of his gloomier predictions have also come true. In the nineteen-thirties, he thought that excessive reliance on fossil fuels — coal, oil and gas — was dangerously short-sighted. He also predicted that in future, wars would be fought over access to water. In arid regions where a single river flows through more than one country, this is certainly moving up the agenda. And he was convinced that humanity's over-dependence on techno-academic motion would dangerously destabilize the planet's weather systems.

The legacy

Viktor Schauberger was one of the remarkable men of the twentieth century. He had insights and appreciations that even now, as we move into the twenty-first century, remain largely unexplored by mainstream science.

His inspiration came from the days when he was a woodsman, with very little contact with the wider world. There, he acquired a deep appreciation of the trees and the water, and a reverence for the living processes of Mother Earth. But he had the woodsman's distrust of the works of Man.

His skill was as an engineer, although a most unusual one. He was able to learn from the processes of Nature around him, and apply his learning to develop machines. Then, given his mistrust of the rest of humanity, he proceeded on a damage-limitation exercise. He would offer alternatives to the most damaging consequence of human civilization as he saw it: its wrong-headed technology. He offered solutions, sticking-plasters, without explaining the underlying system that produced them.

This policy has some obvious flaws. First, from his own experience, he knew that others had difficulty applying his ideas. They could not even build the logging flumes without his help. These were very simple constructions in comparison to his later inventions. One wonders if he realistically expected others to develop his sophisticated machines. Even he himself had to make subtle modifications as he proceeded from drawing-board to prototype, and for him the underlying principles were almost second nature, the result of years of investigation.

Second, people sensed that he was offering the result of his work with very little explanation of the journey to get there. Given his mistrust of and lack of respect for twentieth-century civilization and the people he saw as its upholders, he had no inclination to offer a more thorough explanation. This in turn means that the very people who were best equipped to develop his inventions were unlikely to accept them.

As well as having small chance of acceptance, this policy had an inherent danger. Viktor Schauberger had discovered a way to use some powerful natural processes. Power implies responsibility, and his only way to prevent irresponsible use of his discoveries was to withhold information about them. Others in a similar situation have spent many years training their students to ensure that they apply the knowledge so gained with wisdom and care.

Despite his sincere wish to pass on his knowledge, Viktor Schauberger was not a natural teacher. His mistrust of the motives of schools and universities gave him little appetite to be one. By temperament he was drawn to the practicalities, not the theory that underpinned them. However, he was acutely aware of the importance of his discoveries, and left behind copious writings. He left details of his inventions, and copies of his correspondence. Nonetheless, he never put together his understandings into a coherent system. The only book he wrote did not have an attractive title. *Unsere Sinnlose Arbeit* (Our Senseless Toil) is not a title to attract and encourage readers.

He never found enough people with the ability, patience and open-mindedness to go along with him and develop the underlying principles into a whole that could be understood by others. Towards the end of his life, he clung to the hope that, as he had not found any successors in the present one, future generations would be able to develop the ideas he had discovered.

For me personally, Viktor Schauberger's work is an inspiration. It is one more part of the evidence that humans do not necessarily have to leave a trail of destruction behind them wherever they go. There is more to be discovered. There are other ways to live, constructive ways to co-exist on planet Earth. They are there if we look for them.

Fidus in silvis silentibus — *Faithful to the silent forests (Schauberger family motto)*

A Conversation with
Frau Ingeborg Schauberger

Frau Schauberger is the widow of Walter, Viktor Schauberger's son. She still lives in the family home in Bad Ischl, upper Austria, where this converesation was recorded.

Thank you for agreeing to talk to me about your memories of Viktor Schauberger.
Goethe talked about the difference between poetry and reality. A large poem can come from a small core of reality. I want to tell the reality about Viktor Schauberger as I remember him. There are not many people alive now who knew the real Viktor Schauberger.

Ingeborg Schauberger, 2004 (Photograph: Susanne Prock)

I only knew Viktor for a short time, from 1952 until he died in 1958. I did not spend a lot of time with Viktor. Walter and I lived in Bad Ischl, and he lived in Linz.

He was one of the special men of the twentieth century. But by the time I knew him, he was disappointed about many things. It was always the same, all his life. His ideas always fascinated people, but few people could put it into practice.

How did you meet Walter?

I had two brothers. One died in the second world war. One day his widow, my sister-in-law, said a very interesting man is coming this evening. He talks a lot. Would you like to come too? So I decided to meet this man, and it was Walter. We became friends. I was 36 years old, also a widow. My husband had died in the war, in Russia. Walter was 37, divorced with two children. I met his children, and from the first moment I saw them, I liked them too. This was in 1952.

Walter always said that he would never remarry, and I was also happy to be friends with him. But one day Jörg (her son) announced that he wanted to come to the Earth, and so we changed our minds. Viktor did not come to the wedding. I think maybe Walter forgot to invite him! I remember him asking his mother if Viktor had been invited.

At first, Viktor did not approve of the marriage. His own marriage by this time was not very happy, and he was sceptical about marriage generally. He was a difficult husband. He could be very charming to women when he chose to be, but he said to his wife, Maria, you don't understand my work. Stay in the kitchen and look after the children, that is plenty for you! He did not feel that he had her support. She was seven years younger than him. Her birthday was the day after his. She died twenty years after him, almost to the day.

I did not know if I had Viktor's respect. Later Walter said yes, he respects you. He was charming to me, when we talked together alone.

Walter talked a lot. What did he talk about?
Walter said help Nature, help the trees. We have to have many more trees, more woodland. The first task for the woodland is to bring the water into existence. What can we do for Nature, what can we do for the woods, and what can we do for the woods and the water together? He always talked about this.

This was a time of industrial growth, the time of the German postwar economic miracle. Everything had to be bigger and better. These two men, Viktor and Walter, said it is not good to always have bigger and bigger. They said you have to look, where is the concentration, the essence, what is important for the whole of life. For Viktor and Walter, this was the important thing. How they could put this idea across so that people could understand it.

The Schauberger family has a long tradition of working in the woods. Do any family members do this work still now?
Viktor was the last. He had grown up north of Linz, in an area of original woodland even now. This is rare in Austria these days. He was a soldier for four years in the first world war. He fought in Russia, Italy, Serbia and France, and was wounded. After the war, he worked in the wild woodland until 1924, then his forestry work was finished. After he built the logging flume (his first invention, which brought him to the attention of a wider audience), he was invited to work in Vienna. He was the last one in his family to work in the woods. Now nobody does that work. There is no hunting, nobody works in the wild woodland.

What did Viktor talk about?
Viktor Schauberger always said, think about Nature. Nature has to have a long time to grow. So natural things do not happen immediately. He used to say to Walter, now, everything is more expensive than water. But you will see, the next war will be about oil. And even more than oil, about water.

He always said, 'Can't you see it? Can't you see the water climbing up in the trees, 30 metres or more? There is no pump in the Earth! Nature works silently, without heat or pollution. In industry there is always noise and heat and pollution.'

He said that with the way industrial society has built up, now we are up to our necks in problems, we are drowning in difficulty. What can we do to get humanity back to the right way? He said, who will speak for the water? For the Earth? Nowadays, things are a little better than in Viktor's and Walter's time. The times are turning towards Viktor Schauberger's way of thinking.

He wanted to provoke people, to make them think. He would say to the engineers and professors, you don't know. You can't even tell me how a blade of grass grows. And if you can't tell me that, then what about the trees? Then he would put on his hat and leave.

He was a compelling speaker. When he spoke, everybody listened to him, and they understood what he meant. But when they went away and tried to remember it, the influence diminished. They remembered the feeling, not the understanding. They didn't remember what they had understood when they were in his presence. It was as if a connection had been cut.

He had a group of devoted supporters, who loved to listen to him speak. Afterwards, they would say, that was excellent! But when he asked them what they had understood, their jaws dropped and they said nothing.

He was an impatient man. Sometimes he was angry and frustrated that his life was too short for him to put across all his ideas and the whole of his vision. He said, 'Can't you understand me?' Looking back, I can see that he was unhappy. He spoke and spoke and spoke, and nobody seemed to hear him. It was like talking into thin air. And many of the people who did listen to him, they wanted immediate answers. For Viktor and Walter, the understanding of Nature came first. The machines came much later.

For him, his life's work was to speak to everybody, to make people think. He knew he had to put across the whole of his vision before he died. By the time I knew him, I think he could feel his approaching death. This gave him an extra sense of urgency. He had a very clear vision of what was needed. For him, it was simple. So he was very impatient when people did not understand. I think now that he began to have doubts towards the end of his life. He began to wonder if he had achieved anything at all. His ideas were so simple and evident to him, but nobody else seemed able to grasp them.

The tragedy of Viktor Schauberger was that he was unable to communicate what was so clear to him. He knew that people did not understand, but he never asked if the reason for this was with him. It was always everyone else who was at fault.

Another problem was that he did not trust people. He made everything himself, because he did not trust other people to get it right. I think he was afraid that people would take his ideas and use them wrongly, either through ignorance or intent. His work was so unconventional, so extraordinary, that some people thought it was trickery. This was not helpful.

Viktor and Walter thought the same things. Why did they disagree?
They had the same idea, but father said, sorry, it's my idea! He was often angry with Walter. There was a lot of difficulty between the father and son. Viktor always said, 'Be quiet, you don't understand what I mean!'

Viktor came from intuition. His three older brothers all had an academic education, and were distinguished men. But Viktor did not trust the thinking of people who had studied academically. Viktor believed that a person's thinking is spoilt by academic training. Academic training prevents people from appreciating the ways of Nature.

Walter had studied at the University. Viktor did not like to share his ideas with him. He was afraid that Walter would explain his ideas incorrectly, that he would say things Viktor could not accept.

One day, father was here in Ischl. He and I had a discussion. I said, father, it is not so. Walter knows something too.

Viktor asked me, do you support Walter? I said yes, I stand by him in what he does, and I know that Walter also has an intuitive understanding of the ways of Nature. Viktor reluctantly accepted this, and after that he never said another word against Walter. They worked well together in the end, in the last two or three years of Viktor's life.

In the end, Viktor said to Walter, 'I think it is good that you studied academically. You can speak with the academics, the engineers in their language.' Because nobody understood Viktor's language. They were reconciled, and this made Walter very happy. After that he was more settled.

Walter respected his father and his ideas. Walter would translate his father's ideas in a way that people could understand. Walter was intuitive too. He was the sort of man who could see that a woman was pregnant before she knew it herself! He could bridge the two worlds — he was intuitive and academically fluent. Viktor also bridged two worlds, from that of the old knowledge from his own father to the present. Viktor was a hundred years before his time.

And then there was the American episode.
We don't know the exact background of the American adventure. Nobody knows exactly what happened, and many people speculate about it. In 1958 two men, two Americans came here. They promised Viktor mountains of gold. They said, anything you want, Viktor, you can have. It will be possible to bring it all with you. Come with us to Texas. Viktor understood no English, and Walter only spoke basic English. He was only interested in the language of Mathematics and Physics. There was a translator, a naturalized German-American. He said to me, no word. Don't talk about this to anyone. We are watching you.

First they went to New York. There was an official welcome. 'What luck for America, what luck for you,' they said. They spent three or four days in New York then flew to Dallas. Then they drove out into the desert. They were provided with a bungalow in the desert. And so Viktor and Walter asked, when can we begin to work? You must have time to acclimatize, they said. But there was no work, no target. Walter did not know why they were there. They always had the feeling that they were being controlled.

Viktor became ill and went into the hospital. They did everything possible, anything he wanted, first class treatment. But nobody in the USA told the family in Austria that Viktor was ill. We didn't know he was ill.

He wanted to come back home. They said, if you want to return to Europe, you must sign this document. He had to promise not to speak about his ideas. If he had any new ideas, he was not allowed to speak to anybody about them. Only to the Americans. He was forced to sign this document. Five days after his return, he died. Before he died, he always said I can't say anything. They have taken my words.

After Viktor's death, an American came and apologized to Walter for the way they had been treated. But he couldn't explain why it had happened, either. Later, other Americans came, five or six of them at different times. They all said, you will have to excuse the treatment you had. Not all Americans are so bad. But Walter had nothing to do with Americans after that.

Tell me about Pythagoras-Kepler-System.

Walter started the PKS. He felt that his life's work was to explain the principles behind Viktor's system. Walter studied Kepler's ideas very intensively, and saw the correspondences with Viktor's intuitive insights. He looked for a mathematical explanation of Viktor's system. Kepler's work with the movement of the planets was a good starting point.

And Pythagoras?

Pythagoras is almost too far back in the past, but what he learnt in Egypt also has resonances with Viktor's ideas. Pythagoras was the grandfather, Kepler was the father and Viktor was the

Ingeborg Schauberger and the author, 2004
(Photograph: Susanne Prock)

son. Each picked up the baton from his predecessor and passed it on. With each of them the expression is different, but the core principles are the same.

JÖRG (*her son*): Pythagoras and Kepler were both heroes for my father, as they brought the idea of Harmonics into Physics and Astronomy. They led my father to his Natural Tone Law — Natur-Ton-Gesetz — with hyperbolic cones and the hyperbolic spiral as manifestation of harmonics in evolution. That is why the PKS symbol is a hyperbolic spiral.

I know about Viktor Schauberger's ideas from reading Olof Alexandersson's book, and Callum Coats' translations of his writings. So his message is reaching out to people now.
Olof Alexandersson came here in 1959. He was the first outsider to make connection with Walter. I don't know where the

connection came from. He came here six or seven times, and they kept in contact. He was a great help for us, and still is. Everybody who read his book said, oh, what a man Viktor was! Olof and Walter had an academic relationship. With me, it was a personal friendship.

Callum Coats first came to Bad Ischl one year after Viktor died, with his mother. His mother knew Richard St Barbe Baker, and he introduced her to the Schauberger family. I remember when Callum came. He stepped into the PKS office and saw the spirals drawn on the walls. At that moment, a big door opened for him. It was a life-changing moment. The memory of those spirals stayed with him. Later, he came back and worked here.

Callum is a dear friend of mine. I think that wherever Viktor is, he is very pleased with Callum.

Bad Ischl, Austria, June 3–6, 2004

Sources, Contacts and Applications

Sources and contacts

Groups exploring and implementing Viktor Schauberger's ideas:

PYTHAGORAS-KEPLER-SYSTEM according
to Viktor and Walter Schauberger
Kaltenbach 162, A-4820 Bad Ischl, Austria.
Tel +43 6132 24814
www.pks.or.at

The organization set up by Walter Schauberger, PKS hosts German-language seminars about aspects of Viktor and Walter Schauberger's work. They also host occasional seminars in English. They have open days every Wednesday from May to September, from 4pm to 7pm.

ALICK BARTHOLOMEW
Sulis Health, The Hollies, Mill Hill, Wellow, Bath BA2 8QJ
www.schauberger.co.uk

Publisher Alick Bartholomew first brought Viktor Schauberger's work to the attention of the English-speaking world. His website contains an extensive list of Schauberger-related links.

GRUPPE DER NEUEN 'The New Group'
Dipl.-Ing. Volker Jonas, Dewitzer Str. 103, D-04425 Taucha Germany
Tel.: 034298 49091
http://www.gruppederneuen.de

This group was set up by friends of Walter Schauberger, to further the investigation of Viktor's ideas.

IMPLOSION MAGAZINE

Klaus Rauber, Geroldseckstr. 4, 77736 Zell a.H.

Tel. 07835–5252, Fax: 07835–631498

http://www.implosion-ev.de

This German-language magazine was established in 1958 by Aloys Kokaly, a supporter and friend of Viktor Schauberger, and has been revived by Klaus Rauber.

THE INSTITUTE FOR ECO-TECHNOLOGY

Krokegatan 4, S-413 18 Göteborg, Sweden

http://iet-community.org

Inspired by Viktor Schauberger's ideas, this group explores and encourages practical applications of his work.

VORTEX SCIENCE

www.vortexscience.com

'Harnessing Nature to serve humanity.' This Canadian-based website, run by William Baumgartner and inspired by the work of Viktor Schauberger among others, explores new ways to think about our planet and new non-destructive technologies.

FRANK GERMANO

www.frank.germano.com

Based in the USA, Frank Germano is an engineer, interested in promoting and applying Viktor Schauberger's ideas. He runs an email discussion group, which can be accessed via this site. The group can be accessed directly via *http://groups.yahoo.com/group/viktorschaubergergroup*

MODERN ENERGY RESEARCH LIBRARY

http://merlib.org

Another useful site, based in Finland. Its stated aim is to help others discover the insights and inventions of Viktor Schauberger and others.

Applications

Some commercial applications of Viktor Schauberger's ideas

PKS GARTENGERATE AUS KUPFER
Kaltenbach 162, A-4820 Bad Ischl, Austria.
www.kupferspuren.at
PKS Copper Garden tools, inspired by Viktor Schauberger's work
with copper agricultural implements.

IMPLEMENTATIONS COPPER GARDEN TOOLS
Jane Cobbald
P.O. Box 2568, Nuneaton CV10 9YR, U.K, Tel/fax 0845 330 3148
or +44 24 7639 2497.
www.implementations.co.uk
The UK distributor of PKS Copper Garden Tools

CENTRE FOR IMPLOSION RESEARCH
POB 38, Plympton, Plymouth PL7 5YX, UK
tel +44 (0)1752 345 552, fax +44 (0)1752 338 569
www.implosionresearch.com
Dolly Knight and Jonathan Stromberg have developed a range of
devices to improve the quality of water. They also manufacture personal harmonizers, which have been shown to improve the wearer's
well-being.

VORTEX WATER SYSTEMS
PO Box 1295, Bandera, TX 78003, USA
Tel 830–796–8377, fax 830–796–8033
http://www.texashillcountrymall.com/vortex/
Dan Reese has developed water purification systems based on vortex
technology.

References and Further Reading

— VIKTOR SCHAUBERGER'S WRITINGS

The main sources for Chapters 1 to 11 are the four volumes of the *Eco-Technology Series* (Gateway Press, 1998–2000) representing the writings of Viktor Schauberger translated and edited by Callum Coats:
>Volume One, *The Water Wizard*
>Volume Two, *Nature as Teacher*
>Volume Three, *The Fertile Earth*
>Volume Four, *The Energy Evolution*

— OTHER BOOKS ABOUT VIKTOR SCHAUBERGER

Alexandersson, Olof, *Living Water,* 1982. An inspiring little book, telling the story of Viktor Schauberger and his ideas.

Coats, Callum, *Living Energies,* Gateway Press 1996. A more comprehensive overview of Viktor Schauberger's work.

Bartholomew, Alick, *Hidden Nature, The Startling Insights of Viktor Schauberger,* Floris Books 2003. An accessible account of Viktor Schauberger's system of thinking.

— REFERENCES

CHAPTER 1

For a further description of Viktor Schauberger's activities in the war years: Cook, Nick, *The Hunt for Zero Point,* Arrow Press 2002.

CHAPTER 3

For a description of the remarkable properties of water and the string of astounding coincidences which make it uniquely fit to support carbon-based life: Michael J. Denton: *Nature's Destiny.* The Free Press 1998.

CHAPTER 4

On the adaptation of eggs from water to waterless media:
Batmanghelidj, F, *Your Body's Many Cries for Water,* Tagman
Press 2000.

On page 12. Dr Batmanghelidj makes a similar case for the
development of the human body from species living in a watery
environment, which along the way has acquired strategies to
manage its internal water.

CHAPTER 6

A modern textbook of soil science has this to say about the
importance of energy transfer in the soil (a cation is a positively
charged electrical particle):

> Cation exchange joins photosynthesis as a fundamental
> life-supporting process. Without this property of soils
> terrestrial ecosystems would not be able to retain suf-
> ficient nutrients to support natural or introduced veg-
> etation, especially in the event of such disturbances as
> timber harvest, fire, or cultivation. (From Brady, Nyle
> C. and Weil, Raymond R., *The Nature and Properties
> of Soils,* eleventh edition, Prentice Hall 1996, p.270.)

Half a century earlier, this process was a fundamental part of
Viktor Schauberger's approach to cultivation. It would seem that
mainstream science has caught up with him.

CHAPTER 7

For a description of the chemical elements: Emsley, John,
Nature's Building blocks: An A–Z Guide to the Elements, Oxford
University Press 2001.

The creation of oxygen by sunlight: Viktor Schauberger's
description of oxygen as solidified sunlight borders on the mysti-
cal, but there is a physical explanation for it. Water vapour high in
the atmosphere comes into contact with sunlight energy. With this
energy it breaks down into its constituent hydrogen and oxygen.
The process is known as *photolysis.* The hydrogen is too light to

be retained by the Earth, and so escapes into space. Oxygen, a heavier element, is retained within the Earth's gravity field. So, as a consequence of sunlight meeting the outer atmosphere, there is a net gain of free oxygen for the planet.

For a description of the extraordinary properties of the element carbon, and its fitness for life in the temperature range of liquid water: Denton, *Nature's Destiny,* op. cit., Chapter 5.

On the processes of fermentation: McGee, Harold, *On Food and Cooking: the Science and Lore of the Kitchen,* Harper Collins 1991.

CHAPTER 9

How iron implements drain energy from the soil: Tabraham, A.P., *Solar Energy and Dowsing in the Isles of Scilly for Gardeners and Farmers,* published 1982 by A.P. and E.V. Tabraham, St Mary's, Isles of Scilly.

A.P. Tabraham is an experienced dowser. The book tells of his researches into why an early-flowering narcissus grown in the Scilly Isles was not flowering early any more. Iron implements played a significant part in this, he found.

On copper tools and slugs: Slugs' and snails' blood contains haemocyanin, based on copper, rather than haemoglobin as mammals' blood does. For a further discussion of the significance of this, see *The Story of Copper Garden Tools* by Jane Cobbald, available from Implementations, P.O. Box 2568, Nuneaton CV10 9YR, UK.

CHAPTER 10

There is one book frequently referred to by Viktor Schauberger that I have not been able to locate. This is *The Flight of the Great Horse* by Sven Hedin. According to Viktor Schauberger, this book describes the remarkable technologies still extant in the Middle East at the time of Hedin's visit, for transporting water in underground conduits.

Sven Hedin was a Swedish explorer in the first half of the twentieth century. Other books by him are available, including

descriptions of his travels in the Gobi Desert. Apart from a preoccupation with measuring people's skulls, which was considered a
valid scientific enquiry at the time and has since fallen out of fash-
ion, he was clearly a brave, open-minded and honourable man.

For further reading on Goethe:

Naydler, Jeremy, *Goethe on Science: an anthology of
Goethe's scientific writings,* Floris Books, Edinburgh
1996.

Gray, Ronald, *Goethe: a critical introduction,* Cambridge
University Press 1967.

On Leonardo da Vinci:

Viktor Schauberger frequently alluded to Leonardo's *Primo
Motore.* The only reference to the Prime Mover that I have found
is in Leonardo's notebook now known as the *Codex Atlanticus.*
Here is the section in the original Italian (but not written from
right to left as Leonardo did) followed by a translation:

*Ogni corpo sperico di densa e resistente superfizie,
mosso da pari potenzia farà tanto movimento con sua
balzi causati da duro e solio smalto, quanto a gittarlo
libero per l'aria.*

*O mirabile giustizia di te, Primo Motore! Tu non ài
voluto mancare a nessuna potenzia l'ordini e qualità
de' sua neciessari effetti, con ciò sia che una potenzia
debbe cacciare 100 bracci una cosa vinta da lei, e
quella nel suo obbedire trova intoppo, ài ordinato che
la potenzia del corpo ricusi novo movimento, il quale
per diversi balzi recuperi la intera somma del suo
debito viaggio.*

Every spherical body of thick and resisting surface when
moved by an equal force will make such a movement in the
rebounds caused by its impact on a concrete ground as if it were
thrown freely through the air.

O how admirable is Thy justice, O Thou First Mover!
Thou hast not willed that any power should be
deprived of the processes or qualities necessary for
its results; for, if a force have the capacity of driving
an object conquered by it, a hundred braccia, and
this object while obeying it meets with some obstacle,
Thou hast ordained that the force of the impact will
cause a new movement, which by diverse rebounds
will recover the entire amount of the distance it
should have traversed. (The Notebooks of Leonardo
da Vinci, World's Classics, Oxford University Press
1998, p.76.)

For more about Heraclitus:
Barnes, Jonathan, *Early Greek Philosophy,* Penguin Classics 1987.

CHAPTER 11
A full translation of Professor Popel's report is in *The Energy Evolution,* pp.219–46.
The second half of the chapter is based on information provided by Frau Ingeborg Schauberger.

CHAPTER 12
On water research inspired by Rudolf Steiner:
Schwenk, Theodor, *Sensitive Chaos,* Rudolf Steiner Press, London 1965.
Wilkes, John, *Flowforms,* Floris Books, Edinburgh 2004.

On changing attitudes to the River Rhine:
For more about the 1998 Rhine Action Plan on Flood Defence, see the United Nations Environment Program webpage, *http:// www.unep.org/geo/geo3/english/463.htm*
On changing attitudes to UK woodland: Rackham, Oliver, *The Illustrated History of the Countryside,* Weidenfeld & Nicholson 2003.

Index

Hidden Nature

The Startling Insights of Viktor Schauberger

Austrian naturalist Viktor Schauberger (1885–1958) was far ahead of his time. From his unusually detailed observations of the natural world, he pioneered a completely new understanding of how nature works. He also foresaw, and tried to warn against, the global waste and ecological destruction of our age.

This book describes and explains Schauberger's insights in contemporary, accessible language. His remarkable discoveries — which address issues such as sick water, ailing forests, climate change and, above all, renewable energy — have dramatic implications for how we should work with nature and its resources.

www.florisbooks.co.uk

Understanding Water

Developments from the Work of Theodor Schwenk

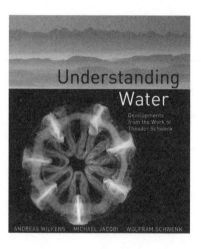

Throughout the ages, people have experienced the life-giving and healing forces in water. Water is integral to life and surrounds us, in nature and in our own bodies. But not all water is the same. Water can carry good energies, and bad energies. How can we understand water enough to know the difference?

Theodor Schwenk, the renowned author of Sensitive Chaos, founded an institute for water research in the Black Forest in Germany. He developed the Drop Picture Method, which displays the characteristics of water clearly for the non-specialist. Today, the Institute continues his work and here presents momentous findings about the quality of our drinking water, groundwater, spring water and river water.

This book offers a unique insight into the world of water.

www.florisbooks.co.uk